# *Interactive*

# BIBLE

# Bulletin Boards

## Fall

by Susan Julio
and
Cindy Schooler

**These pages may be copied.**

**Permission is granted** to the buyer of this book to reproduce, duplicate or
photocopy these student materials for use with pupils in
Sunday school or Bible teaching classes.

Rainbow Books

Rainbow Publishers • P.O. Box 261129 • San Diego, CA 92196

# ✳ Dedication ✳

To my friends, family, and especially in memory of my grandmother Gaye B. Jarrett. My memories of walking to the bookmobile together, reading stories aloud, and her open Bible on the dining room table instilled a love for books in me at an early age. Thanks, Grandma. I still miss you. —C.S.

INTERACTIVE BIBLE BULLETIN BOARDS FOR FALL
©1999 by Rainbow Publishers, fourth printing
ISBN 1-885358-32-6
Rainbow reorder #RB36711

Rainbow Publishers
P.O. Box 261129
San Diego, CA 92196

Illustrator: Joel Ryan
Editor: Christy Allen
Design: Stray Cat Studio, San Diego, CA

*Printed in the United States of America*

# Interactive BIBLE Bulletin Boards

## ✳ Contents ✳

# Interactive BIBLE Bulletin Boards

## ✳ Introduction ✳

Bulletin boards can be fun, involve your students and use easy-to-find supplies, plus look great and offer solid Bible-teaching. That's why *Interactive Bible Bulletin Boards* was created: to provide the materials you need to make bulletin boards that you can use to teach about God. Each of the four seasonal books in the *Interactive Bulletin Board* series contains 13 bulletin boards for preschoolers and 13 bulletin boards for elementary-age kids. Just one book has enough bulletin board patterns and ideas for your church's entire children's department!

The best part about this book is that all of the bulletin boards either involve the children in creating them—allowing you more time to spend on teaching—or involve them with learning manipulatives that you display. Either way, you will quickly construct exciting bulletin boards that reach kids.

Each bulletin board is a lesson, including:

| | |
|---|---|
| ✳ Plan | the lesson's objective |
| ✳ Memorize | an age-based memory verse |
| ✳ Gather | a supply list |
| ✳ Prepare | pre-class tasks for you to complete |
| ✳ Create | step-by-step instructions |
| ✳ Teach | ideas to extend the lesson |

You will also find all of the patterns for each bulletin board, plus borders and lettering to complete the board's look. Tips on pages 6-9 will help you make the most of the book, as well as your supplies and creativity.

The bulletin boards in this book are unique. They were created out of a desire to see children using the bulletin board as an extension to teaching a biblical concept. These boards say, "Yes, please touch" in a world that tells children, "No, don't touch." The children in your classroom will love the new experience you are about to give them.

# ✳ How to Create Beautiful Bulletin Boards Using the Materials in This Book ✳

Each of the 26 Bible-teaching, interactive bulletin boards in this book contains complete instructions, patterns, lettering and borders to put the bulletin board together, plus teaching hints to use the board with your class. The following pages will offer you ideas for your bulletin boards and explain how to best use the book.

## ✳ Backgrounds

Each bulletin board in this book includes suggestions for background colors—most people use poster paper or construction paper. You may want to select a background that will work with board designs you will use throughout the season. Also, feel free to experiment with materials of your choice to add background interest, such as:

- ✳ Textured fabrics: felt, flannel, burlap, fur, cheesecloth
- ✳ Paper or plastic tablecloths
- ✳ Gift wrap
- ✳ Cotton batting
- ✳ Newspaper
- ✳ Brown paper bags crumpled and then flattened
- ✳ Maps
- ✳ Crepe paper
- ✳ Colored tissue paper
- ✳ Wallpaper
- ✳ Self-stick plastic in colors or patterns
- ✳ Shelf paper
- ✳ Colorful corrugated paper available from school supply stores
- ✳ Poster board on which figures may be permanently attached

## ✳ Making Bulletin Boards Three-Dimensional

Although bulletin boards are normally flat, there are many imaginative ways to add a three-dimensional effect to them. Many of the bulletin boards in this book already include ideas for three-dimensional effects, but there are others you may want to try:

✳ Place cork, cardboard or foam behind figures or letters.

✳ Attach large figures to the bulletin board by curving them slightly outward from the board.

✳ Glue or attach three-dimensional objects such as cotton balls, pieces of wood, twigs, nature items, feathers, yarn, toys, small clothing objects (like scarves and mittens), balloons, artificial flowers or leaves, chenille wire, fabrics, corrugated paper, sandpaper, crumpled aluminum foil or grocery bags, rope, plastic drinking straws—the list can go on and on!

✳ "Stuff" figures by putting crumpled newspaper or paper towels behind the figures before attaching them to the bulletin board.

✳ Flowers may be made from individual egg carton sections by cutting off the sections and painting, coloring or decorating them as desired.

✳ Heavy objects may be mounted in the following way: Cut two or more strips of bias binding tape or ribbon (available from fabric stores). Securely staple one end of the bias tape to the bulletin board, place around the item to be mounted and staple the other end (above the object) to the bulletin board so the object hangs securely on the bias tape strips.

## ✳Lettering

This book includes full-sized lettering which is intended to be used on the bulletin boards that you create. To use the lettering, you may do the following:

✳ Trace the lettering onto colored construction paper, cut out each letter and mount them individually on the bulletin board.

✳ Duplicate the lettering onto any paper. Then place that page over the sheet of paper out of which you want to cut the letters. Cut through both sheets using scissors or a craft knife. Mount the letters individually on the bulletin board.

✳ Duplicate the lettering onto white paper and color in the letters with markers.

✳ Duplicate the lettering onto white or colored paper. Cut the words apart and mount each word on the bulletin board in strip form.

✳ Trace the lettering onto paper of any color using colored markers. Cut out the individual letters or cut apart the words and use them in strip form.

✳ Cut the individual letters out of two colors of paper at once. When mounting the letters on the bulletin board, lay one color on top of the other and offset the bottom letter slightly so it creates a shadow effect.

Attractive lettering can also be made by cutting letters out of wallpaper, fabrics, felt, self-stick plastic in colors and patterns, gift wrap, grocery bags, newspapers and other materials. For a professional look, outline letters with a dark marker for a neat edge and good contrast. Always try to use dark colors for lettering, unless the background requires a contrasting color.

Textures may be used for lettering also, either by cutting the letters out of textured materials or by gluing on glitter, sequins, straw, twigs, yarn, rope, lace, craft sticks, chenille wire or other materials.

To mount the letters flat, staple them to the board, use double-sided tape or roll a small piece of tape to make it double-sided. Always put the tape under the letter so it does not show.

Stagger the letters, arch them, dip them or make them look like stair steps or a wave by variegating one letter up and one letter down. Be a non-conformist when it comes to letter placement! Curve your lettering around the board, place your title down one side or across the bottom. Your title doesn't always have to be across the top of the bulletin board.

# ✴ Duplicating Patterns and Lettering

All patterns, lettering and borders in this book may be used right out of the book or traced, enlarged, reduced, duplicated or photocopied to make your bulletin board.

The easiest way to duplicate the materials in this book is to use a copy machine to simply copy the patterns, lettering or borders onto white or colored copy machine paper. For a nominal price you can copy onto colored paper at most copy centers. Construction paper works well in some copy machines.

You may also trace the materials in this book onto white or colored paper by holding the page you wish to trace up to a window or by using carbon paper.

Another way to enlarge items is with an overhead projector. Trace the items you wish to enlarge onto a transparency sheet, then project the image onto a sheet of paper attached to a wall. Adjust the projector until the image is the size you desire and trace the image onto the paper.

# ✴ Mounting Materials onto Your Bulletin Board

It is important that all materials stay securely on your bulletin board until you wish to take them down. This book does not specify how to mount most materials so you may choose the method that works best for your situation.

Stapling materials directly to the bulletin board is the most secure method of mounting most materials and the staples are virtually unnoticeable. Be sure to have a staple remover handy both when you are creating the board and when you are taking it down.

Staples are much better for bulletin boards for small children as it is quite difficult to pull a staple out of a bulletin board, unlike push pins and tacks. Make certain that no loose staples are left on the floor after you finish working on the bulletin board.

Pins may be used if you wish to support the materials rather than make holes. Double-sided tape, or tape rolled to make it double-sided, is also effective. For heavier materials, use carpet tape or packing tape.

# ✴ How to Make Your Bulletin Boards Durable and Reusable

Cover both sides of your bulletin board figures—especially those that will be manipulated by the children—with self-stick plastic. Cut around the figures, leaving a ¼" edge of plastic. (If one figure is made up of several parts, put the parts together before covering with plastic.) You may also glue figures to colored construction paper and cut around them, leaving a narrow border of construction paper.

Also laminate the captions and borders to use again. Take a picture of your completed bulletin board for future color references and diagrams. Glue the developed picture to the outside of a large manila envelope and store the laminated pieces of the bulletin board inside.

# ✴ Teaching with the Bulletin Boards

Each of the bulletin boards in this book includes a suggested memory verse and teaching tips to help you use the bulletin boards to teach important biblical concepts to children.

On those that are designed for the children to assist you in the board's creation, you will find that the students delight in helping and seeing their work on the board. The boards that you create for the children to use in learning will also intrigue and engage them. Almost all of the boards that the children will help you to create require scissors and a few other easy-to-obtain items. A list of materials is included with each board.

Since the titles for these bulletin boards were chosen to encourage a learning concept, they are important to the overall interaction with the bulletin board. The first week that each new bulletin board is displayed, read the titles aloud to the children—especially preschoolers—and explain what it means. Also, show the children how to interact with the board. If you take time at the beginning of the class to introduce the board, you won't have as many individual questions to answer during your lesson. Memory verses were purposely not included on most of the finished bulletin boards for preschoolers since they cannot read, but your continued verbal repetition of the verses will make them familiar to the students.

Bulletin boards are great teaching tools. Besides being obvious colorful additions to a classroom, they can also be used in the following ways:

* Reinforce the lesson
* Improve fine motor skills
* Serve as the focal point of classroom
* Review the previous week's lesson
* Introduce new topics
* Encourage new skills (such as following a maze, turning wheels, opening flaps, etc.)
* Keep and encourage attendance
* Enhance self-image by displaying work
* Encourage interaction with other children

These bulletin boards are unique because they encourage the children to interact with them in some way. Whether the board displays their own work, helps record attendance or allows them to move objects around, the children are encouraged to interact with the bulletin board each time they come into the classroom.

## * Visitors

Be sure to create a few extras of each child-specific item so that visitors will have copies. Your new students will feel more welcome if they know you are prepared for them.

## * A Special Note to Preschool Teachers

The best way to organize a classroom for toddlers is down on your knees! Remember that these are little people, so make sure all of your displays are at their eye level. Lower the bulletin board if possible. Make sure the children can easily reach the interactive activities you create with this book.

## ✳ Borders

Borders are the frame of your bulletin board. Just as you carefully choose an appropriate frame for a picture on the wall, you should choose a border that will enhance your bulletin board. Several border patterns are provided on the following pages for use with selected bulletin boards in this book.

The easiest method for creating and duplicating borders is decribed below. Simply measure the top, bottom and sides of your board (write down the measurements so you will have them the next time you are making a border). Then follow the directions for instant borders. Cut, fold and trace as many strips as you need for your board based on your measurements. You may use colored paper for the borders or copy the patterns onto white paper and have the children color them in with markers.

Glue or tape the border lengths together. Use double-faced tape to attach the border directly to the frame, or staple the border to the edge of the bulletin board. Roll the border to store for future use.

Attractive borders may also be made with the following materials:

* Artificial flowers, leaves or nature items
* Rope or twine
* Braided yarn
* Wide gift wrap ribbon
* Corrugated borders from school supply stores
* Twisted crepe paper streamers
* Christmas tree garland
* Aluminum foil

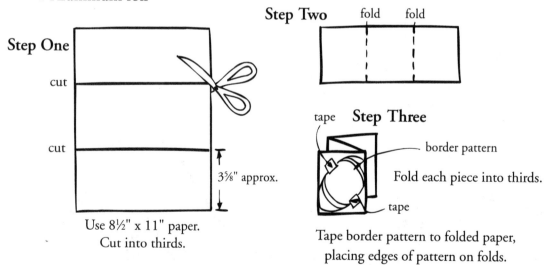

**Step One**

cut

cut

3⅝" approx.

Use 8½" x 11" paper.
Cut into thirds.

**Step Two**   fold   fold

**Step Three**   tape

tape

border pattern

Fold each piece into thirds.

Tape border pattern to folded paper,
placing edges of pattern on folds.

**Step Four**

Cut out pattern. Leave edges that touch folds uncut.

Borders will look
like this:

# ✳ Border Patterns ✳

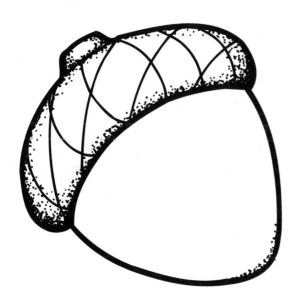

acorn border

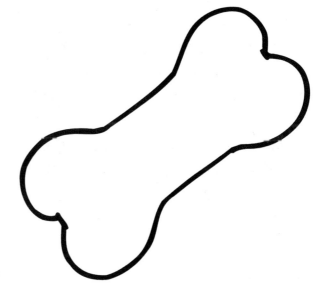

bone border

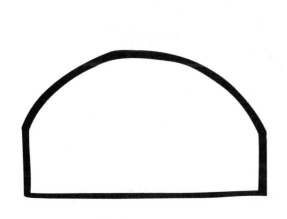

semi-circle border

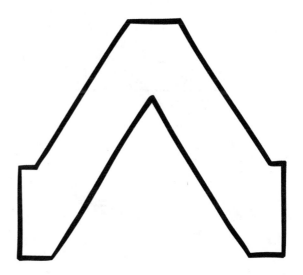

V-shaped border

# ✳ Border Patterns ✳

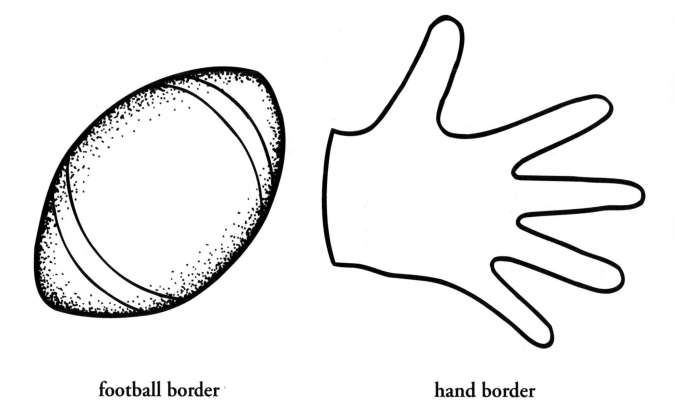

football border

hand border

feather border

pumpkin border

# ✴ Border Patterns ✴

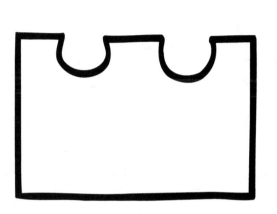

stamp border

heart border

leaf border

leaf border (optional)

### ✳ Plan

To assure that Jesus knows us and loves us.

### ✳ Memorize

*I am the good shepherd.* John 10:14

### ✳ Gather

- patterns for sheep and ears from p. 15
- pattern for lettering from p. 16
- pattern for semi-circle border from p. 11
- poster paper, green
- construction paper, white, yellow and black
- artificial flowers
- marker, black
- poster board, white
- cotton balls
- glue
- crayons

### ✳ Prepare

Duplicate the lettering on yellow paper, one sheep per student on white paper and the sheep ears on black paper. Cut out two ears for each student.

### ✳ Create

1. Cover the board with green paper. Cut out and post the lettering.
2. Show how to cut out the sheep and trace around it on white poster board. Help the children write their names in the middle of their sheep and cut them out.
3. Allow the students to color the sheep's legs black. Then have them glue cotton balls on the sheep. Encourage them to spread out the cotton.
4. Have the students glue the ears on the sheep.
5. While the students work on their sheep, make a white picket fence on the board by criss-crossing white strips of paper along the lower edge. Staple artificial flowers along the bottom of the fence.
6. Cut and accordion-fold strips of yellow paper according to the border directions on p. 10. Trace the semi-circle border pattern and cut out. Attach the border to the board's edges. Students who finish their sheep may assist you in creating the border.
7. Attach the completed sheep to the board.

### ✳ Teach

Ask, We are all new in this class today, but some of you already know one another, don't you? Have you ever been in a situation when you really didn't know anyone else, like a new class at school? How did you feel? Jesus tells us that He knows each one of us. He knows everything about us! So the next time you feel alone, remember that Jesus knows and loves you more than anyone else. Read the Parable of the Lost Sheep from Matthew 18:10-14 to the class.

Suggested Usage: Back-to-school

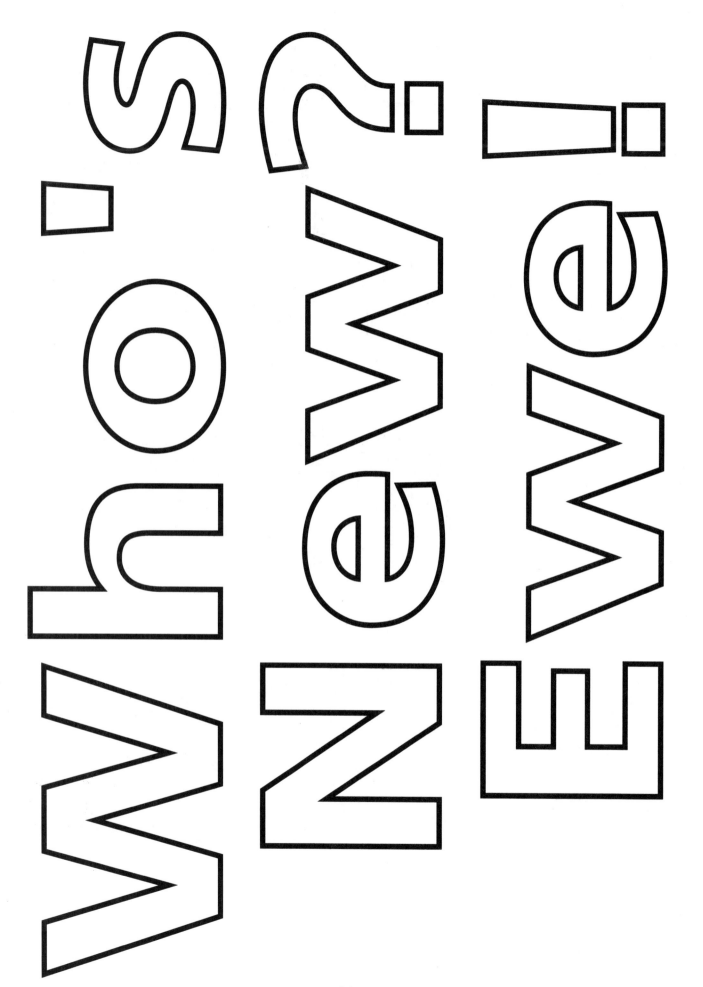

who's ewe! ewe!

WE! E!

## * Plan
To show the beauty of creation in nature and in us.

## * Memorize
*I am fearfully and wonderfully made.* Psalm 139:14

## * Gather
- patterns for leaves from p. 18
- pattern for lettering from p. 19
- pattern for leaf border from p. 13
- construction paper, fall colors
- poster paper, blue, green and brown
- yarn, yellow
- marker, black
- clear self-stick plastic
- Velcro
- push pin
- plastic sandwich bag

## * Prepare
Freehand draw and cut a tree from brown poster paper that comfortably fits your bulletin board. Use the leaf patterns to make one leaf for each child in your class plus extras. Duplicate the lettering on yellow paper.

## * Create
1. Post blue paper on the bulletin board for the sky and green paper to represent the grass.
2. Cut and fold construction paper strips according to the instant border directions on page 10. Trace the leaf pattern onto the folded paper and cut out. Attach the border.
3. Cut a semi-circle wedge from yellow paper for a sun. Cut pieces of yellow yarn and staple them around the sun for rays. Attach the sun.
4. Cut out the colored leaves. Attach the tree trunk to the middle right of the board.
5. Cut out the lettering and attach it to the board.
6. Staple some of the colored leaves to the tree, reserving a leaf for every child in your class.
7. Write each child's name on one of the extra leaves. Cover with self-stick plastic for durability. Stick a piece of Velcro on the backs of the leaves and on the tree.
8. Pin the sandwich bag to the the board to hold the leaves when they are not in use.
9. Use the bulletin board as an attendance chart by having the children place their leaves on the board each week.

## * Teach
Discuss the different leaves and how God made people different, too. Say, **See how some of the leaves are different ? God was creative when He made humans, too! Some of us have blond or black or red hair. Some have light and some have darker skin. But God loves each one of us the same.**

Suggested Usage: Early Fall

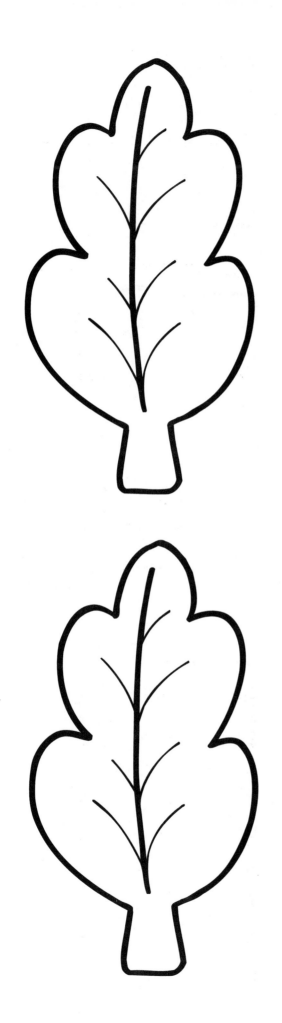

18

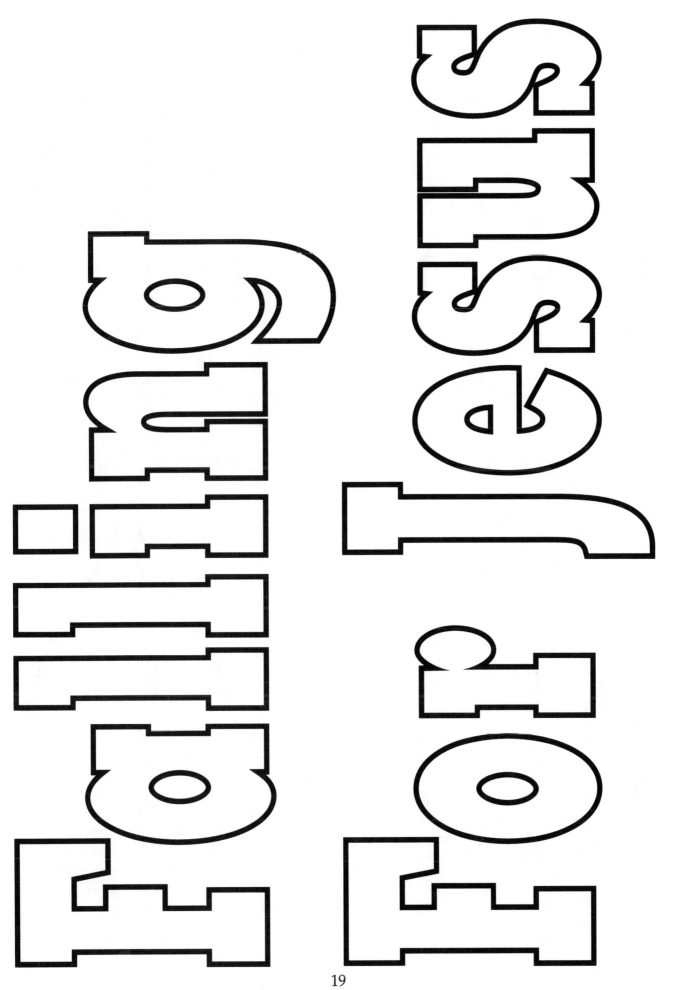

Falling Jesus For

## * Plan

To identify God as the source of physical and spiritual food.

## * Memorize

*I am the bread of life.* John 6:35

## * Materials

• pattern for Bible from p. 21
• pattern for lettering from pp. 22-23
• pattern for hand border from p. 12
• construction paper, skin colors
• markers
• felt, red
• poster paper, yellow
• glue
• cup hooks, self-adhesive
• baskets, plastic berry
• plastic sandwich bags, pint-sized
• crackers

## * Prepare

Duplicate the Bible pattern on white paper and color with markers. Trace a bookmark on red felt. Duplicate the lettering on black paper.

## * Create

1. Attach the yellow poster paper to the board. Post the lettering on the board.
2. Cut and fold strips of skin-colored paper accord-ing to the instant border directions on page 10. Trace the hand border pattern onto the folded paper and cut out. Staple the border around the board's edges.
3. Cut out the Bible and bookmark. Glue the bookmark to the center of the Bible. Attach the Bible to the middle left of the board.
4. Attach the cup hooks to the board.
5. Hang the plastic berry baskets from the hooks.
6. Fill the sandwich bags with crackers and place the bags in the berry baskets on the board.
7. Allow the children to get a cracker each week from the baskets for their snack.

## * Teach

Ask, **What is your favorite food? Why is it impor-tant to eat? In our memory verse, Jesus tells us that He is like bread. That means if we follow Him and learn from the Bible, we will be strong and healthy Christians, just like when we eat bread and other good food that makes our bodies strong and healthy. Let's be thankful that we have enough food to eat for our bodies and that we have God's Word, the Bible, to feed us and help us be good Christians.**

Suggested Usage: Early Fall; harvest time

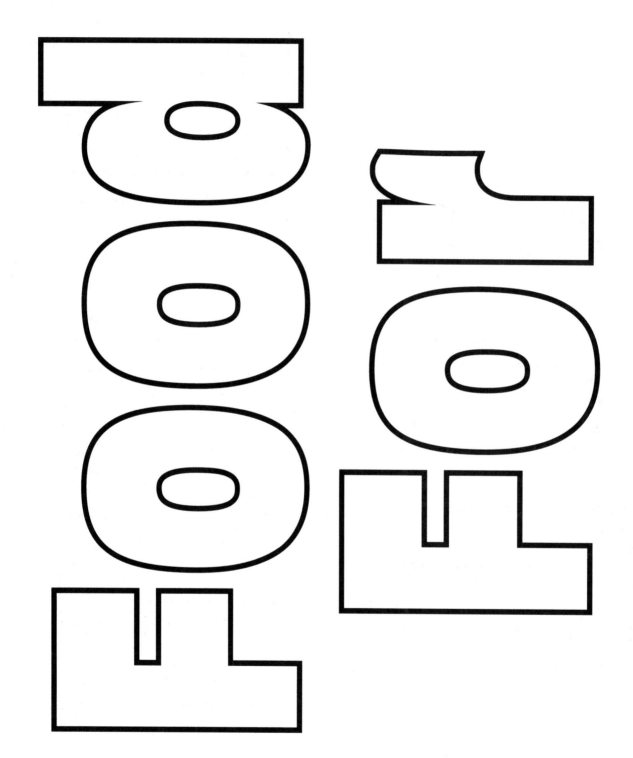

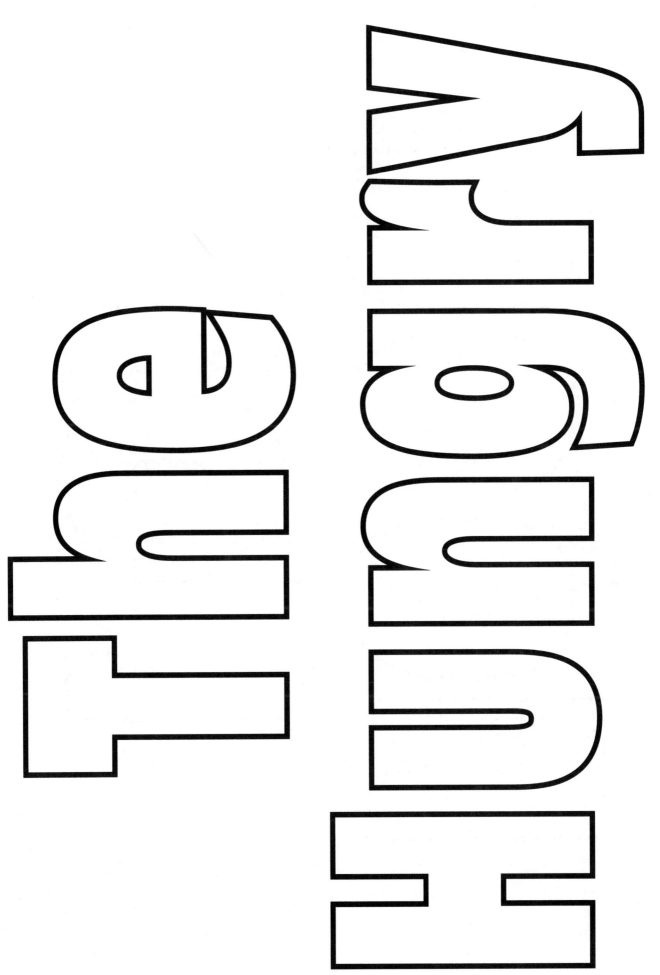

The Hungry

God's Creation Is Good

## * Ages 2-5 *

### * Plan
To reinforce that God purposely created us to be perfectly different.

### * Memorize
*God made the wild animals.* Genesis 1:25

### * Gather
- patterns for barn, silo and animals from pp. 25-28
- pattern for lettering from pp. 29-30
- pattern for hand border from p. 12
- construction paper, various colors
- poster paper, blue and green
- glue
- markers

### * Prepare
Duplicate the barn building and the silo on red paper, the barn roof on brown paper and the silo roof on white paper. Duplicate the animals, hay and corn on appropriate colors of paper. Duplicate the lettering on brown paper.

### * Create
1. Attach the blue paper to the board for the sky and the green paper for the grass. Cut out the lettering and attach it to the board.
2. Cut and fold strips of construction paper according to the instant border directions on page 10. Trace the hand border on the folded paper and cut out. Staple the border around the board's edges.

3. Cut out the barn and use a dark marker to fill in the details on it. Cut three sides of the barn's doors and windows and gently fold them open. Cut the door to the hayloft along three sides and fold it back. Attach the barn to the board.
4. Cut out the farm animals, hay and corn. Glue the farm animals to the board behind the doors. Glue the hay to the barn behind the hayloft door. Be careful not to glue the doors shut!
5. Cut out the silo and its roof. Cut the silo door on three sides and gently fold it open on the uncut side. Attach the silo to the board and glue the corn to the silo behind its door.
6. The children may open and close the three doors.

### * Teach
Call out names of animals and have the students act out the animals. Say, **Even though God made each of these animals different, they are all His creation. And even though each of us is different, we are all His creation, too. He loves each one of us! Aren't you glad God made us with different abilities so we can help each other? Let's remember to love everyone because we know that God planned to make us different.**

Suggested Usage: Early fall; harvest time

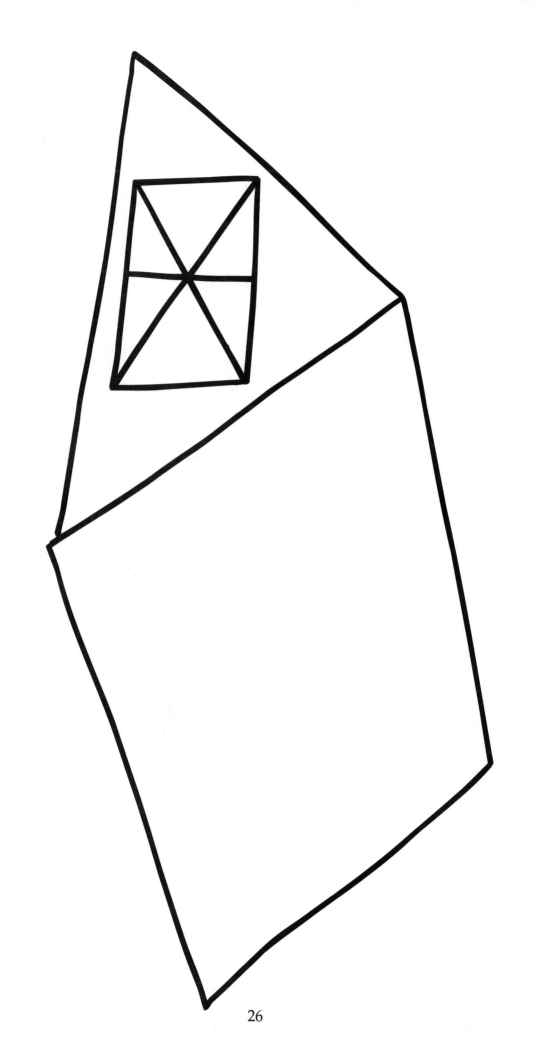

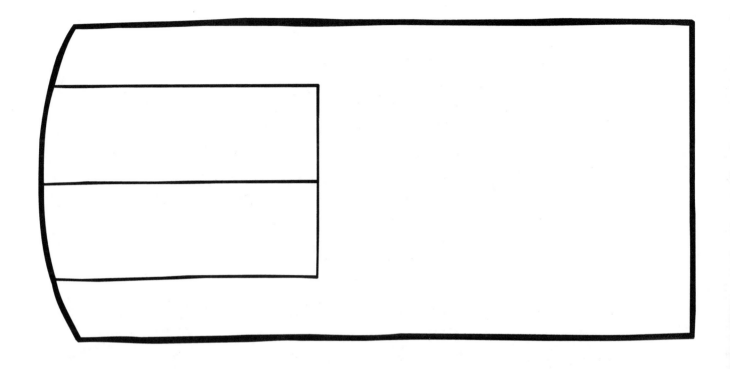

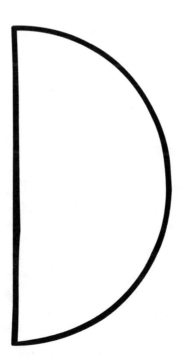

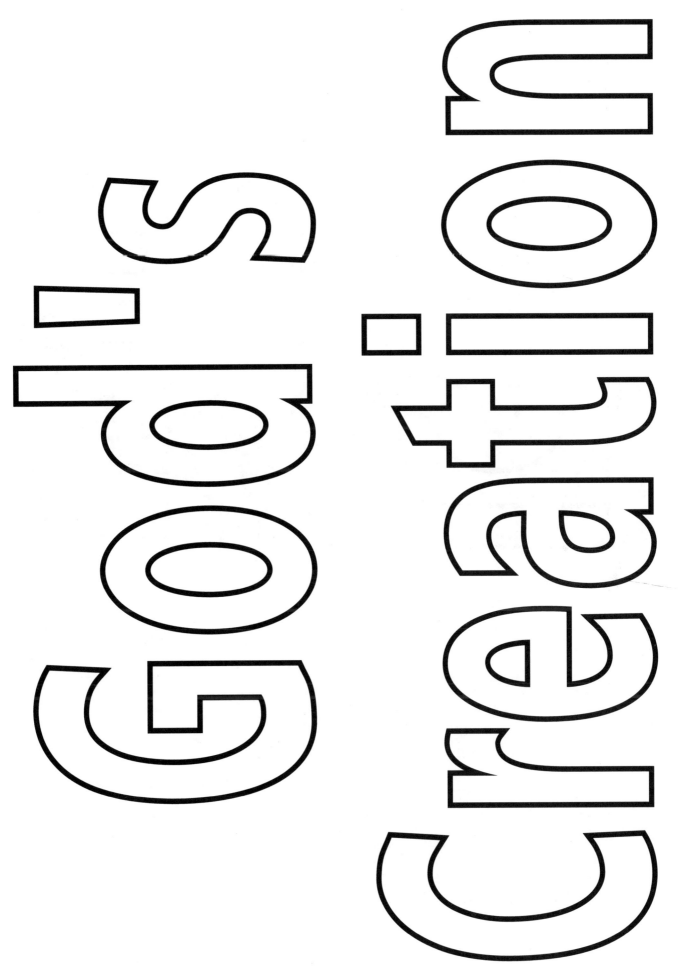

God's Creation

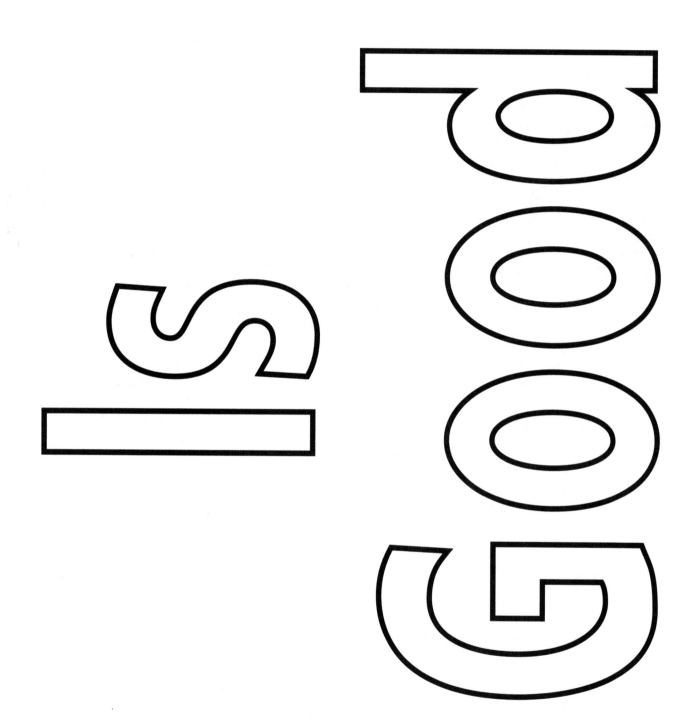

God Is Good

# Harvest of Blessings

## * Plan
To explain why we are commanded to share the gospel.

## * Memorize
*Ask the Lord to send out workers into his harvest field.* Matthew 9:38

## * Gather
- pattern for pumpkin and leaf from p. 32
- pattern for lettering from p. 33
- pattern for leaf border from p. 13
- construction paper, orange, green and brown
- poster paper, yellow and green
- marker, black
- glue
- raffia, brown
- fabric or scarf
- yarn, green
- stickers

## * Prepare
Duplicate two pumpkins for each child on orange paper. Duplicate the lettering on brown paper and the leaves on green paper.

## * Create
1. Attach the yellow paper to the board. Post green background paper to the bottom half of the board for grass. Cut out and attach the lettering.
2. Cut and fold strips of paper according to the instant border directions on page 10. Trace the leaf pattern onto the folded paper and cut out. Staple the border around the board's edges.
3. Cut out the pumpkins. Write each child's name on a pumpkin. Place each pumpkin with a name on top of a plain pumpkin and slightly glue them together at the stem. Make extras for new students who may visit your class.
4. While the glue dries, bunch the raffia lengthwise and tie it with the fabric about ⅓ from the top. Make a bow with the tied fabric and attach the raffia to the bulletin board, on the "grass."
5. Gently bend the dried pumpkins upward. Attach them to the bulletin board by stapling the bottom pumpkin to the board.
6. Make "vines" out of the green yarn by draping it from one pumpkin to the next and stapling.
7. Cut out and post leaves on each pumpkin.
8. Each week, have the children place a sticker inside their pumpkins to mark attendance.

## * Teach
Ask, **What is a harvest? What kinds of things are harvested? Did you know that each week you come to church you are a part of God's harvest? Just like the farmer goes into the field to pull out all of those good things for us to eat, those who follow God are chosen by Him to live forever in heaven.**

Suggested Usage: Harvest theme

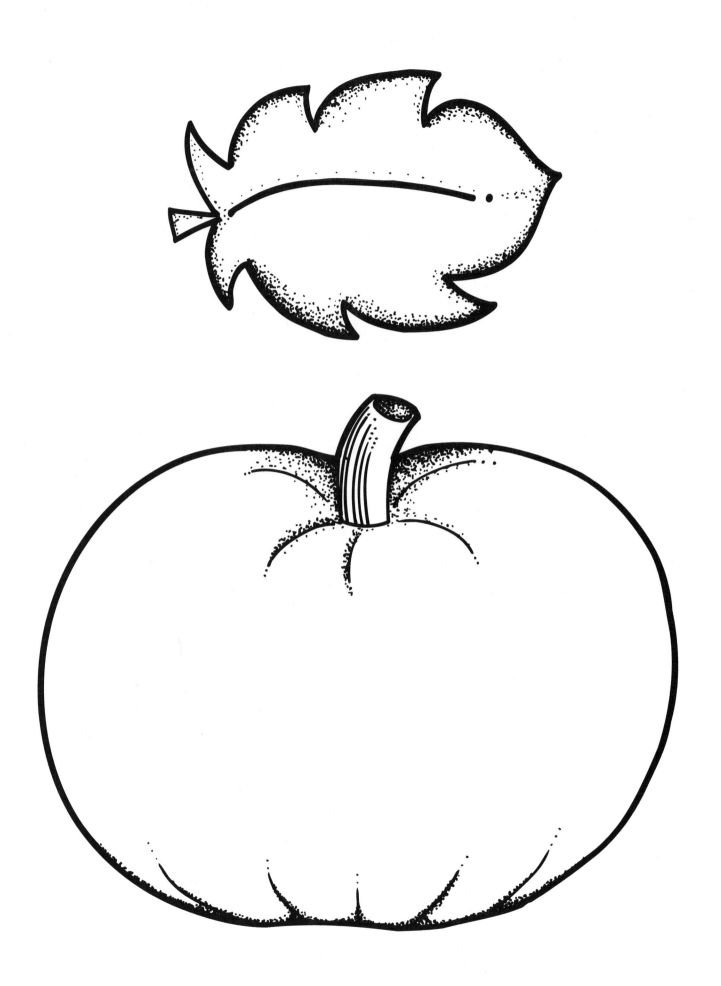

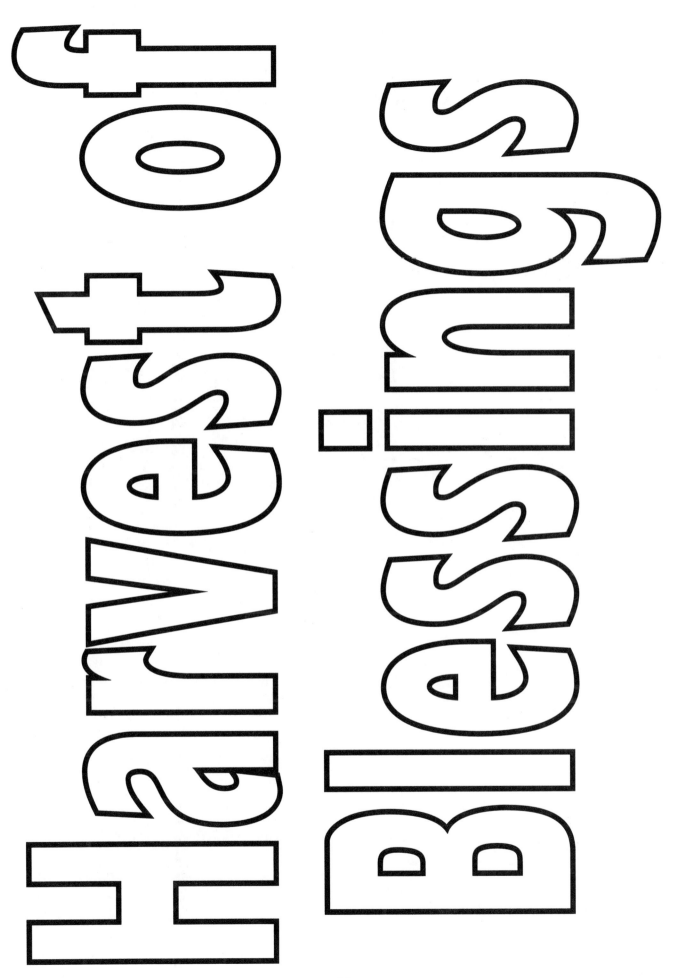

Harvest of Blessings

# Harvest Time

The harvest is plentiful but the workers are few. Matthew 9:37

## ✳ Ages 6-10 ✳

### ✳ Plan

To understand God's call to share the gospel.

### ✳ Memorize

*The harvest is plentiful but the workers are few.*
Matthew 9:37

### ✳ Gather

- pattern for lettering from p. 38
- patterns for cornucopia, fruit and vegetables from pp. 35-37
- pattern for leaf border from p. 13
- poster paper, white
- construction paper, orange, light and dark brown
- paper, white
- marker, black
- scissors
- crayons

### ✳ Prepare

Duplicate the lettering on orange construction paper. Duplicate one cornucopia for each student on light brown construction paper, one circle on dark brown construction paper and several copies of the fruit and vegetables on white paper.

### ✳ Create

1. Cover the bulletin board with white paper. Cut out the lettering and attach it to the top center of the board. Use a black marker to write the memory verse at the bottom of the board.
2. Cut and fold dark brown and orange construction paper strips according to the instant border directions on page 10. Trace the leaf border pattern onto the folded paper and cut out the border. Attach the border around the edges of the board.
3. Distribute the cornucopias, circles and fruit and have the students cut out all of the pieces. Show how to glue the circle on the cornucopia.
4. Allow the students to color the fruit and vegetables. On each piece, have them write the name of a non-believer for whom they could pray and with whom they could share the gospel. Have them glue the produce to the cornucopia.
5. Attach the cornucopias to the board.

### ✳ Teach

Read the memory verse, then ask, **What is a harvest? What are workers? For what kind of harvest is God hoping? How can we be workers in God's harvest?**

Suggested Usage: Harvest theme

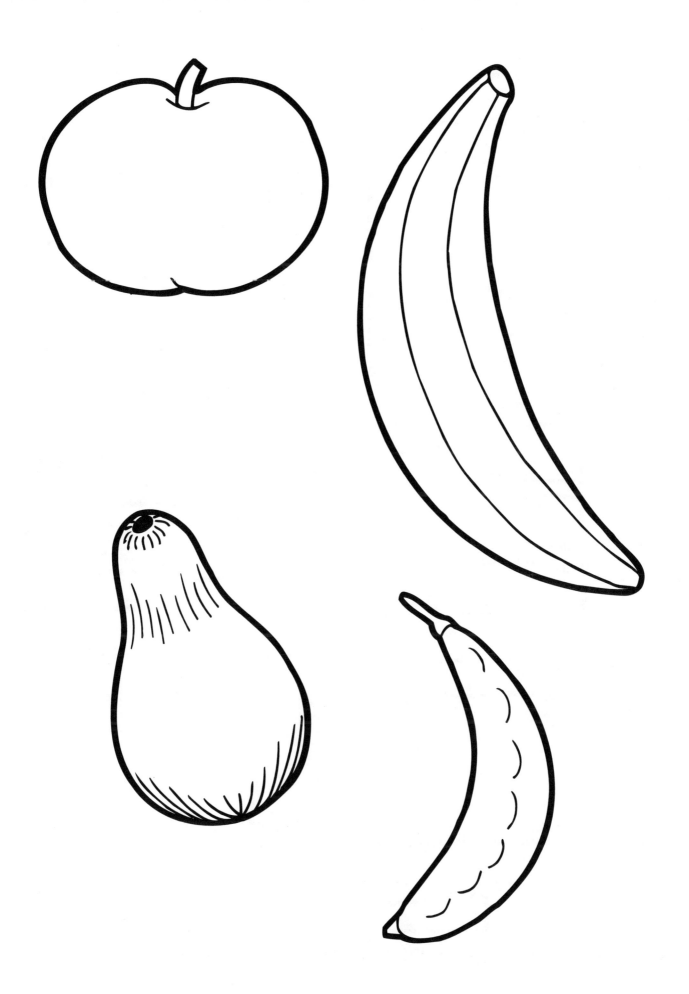

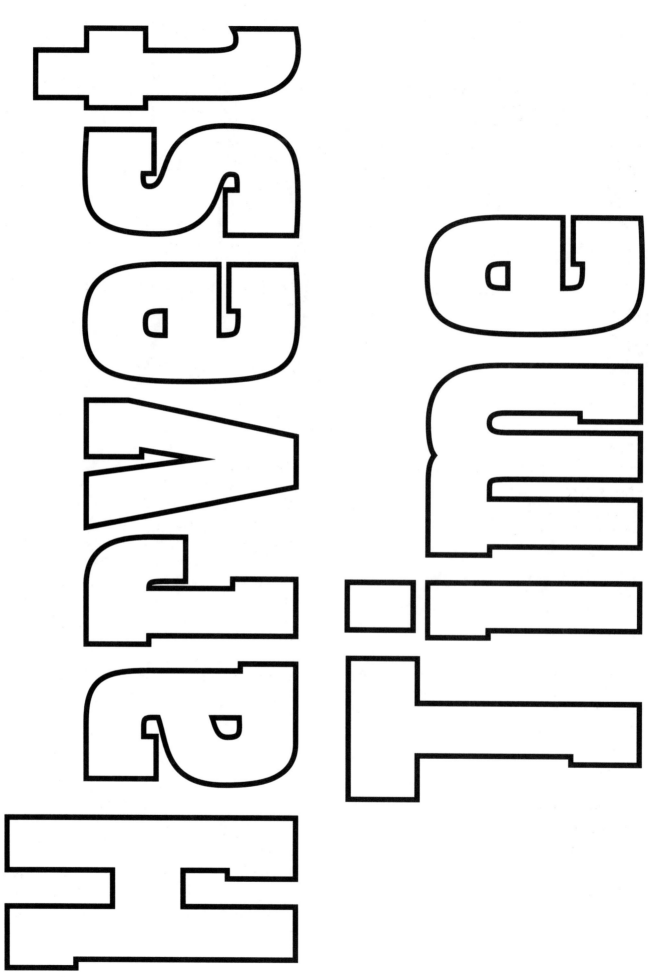

Harvest Time

**✳ Ages 6-10 ✳**

## ✳ Plan
To realize the importance of Christian actions.

## ✳ Memorize
*Every good tree bears good fruit, but a bad tree bears bad fruit.* Matthew 7:17

## ✳ Gather
- pattern for autumn leaves from p. 40
- pattern for leaf border from p. 13
- pattern for lettering from p. 41
- poster paper, blue and green
- tempera paint, brown
- paint brush
- construction paper, fall colors and green
- marker, black
- clear, self-stick plastic
- Velcro
- push pin
- plastic sandwich bag
- silk autumn leaves (optional)

## ✳ Prepare
Duplicate the lettering on red paper and fourteen leaves on various fall colors of construction paper.

## ✳ Create
1. Cover the bulletin board with blue and green paper. Use brown paint to create a large tree in the center of the board (see illustration above).

Allow to dry.
2. Cut out the lettering and attach it to the board. Cut and fold strips of red, orange and yellow construction paper according to the instant border directions on page 10. Trace the leaf border pattern onto the folded paper and cut out the border. Staple the border around the edges of the board. Or, purchase silk autumn leaves and staple around the edges of the board.
3. Cut out the leaves. Write one word of the memory verse on each leaf. Laminate the leaves with the self-stick plastic and attach a tab of Velcro to the back of each. Store the leaves in a plastic sandwich bag attached with a push pin to the lower right hand corner of the board.
4. Attach the corresponding pieces of Velcro to the tree. Challenge the students to arrange the leaves to form the Mystery Verse.

## ✳ Teach
Say, **In addition to leaves, some trees bear (or give) fruit, like the tree mentioned in our memory verse. What kinds of fruit come from trees? What makes some fruit good and some fruit bad? God says we should all try to be trees that bear good fruit. In what ways can we bear good fruit for God?**

Suggested Usage: Early fall

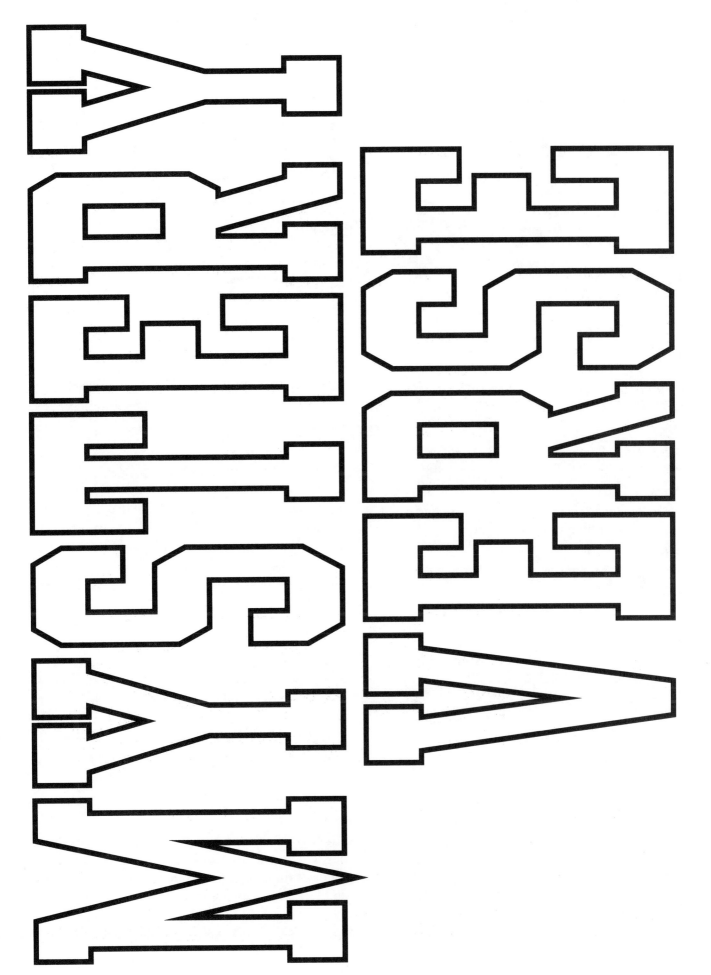

## ✱ Plan

To teach that good actions make God happy.

## ✱ Memorize

*If anything is excellent or praiseworthy—think about such things.* Philippians 4:8

## ✱ Gather

- patterns for tractor, wagon and hay bale from pp. 43-48
- pattern for half-circle border from p. 11
- pattern for lettering from pp. 49-50
- construction paper, brown, black, green, yellow and red
- poster paper, blue and green
- clear, self-stick plastic
- marker, black
- hole punch
- paper fasteners

## ✱ Prepare

Duplicate the tractor on red paper; the wagon on brown paper; eight hay bales on yellow paper; three large wheels, one small wheel and the lettering on black paper; and three additional large wheels and one small wheel on green paper.

## ✱ Create

1. Attach blue paper on the bulletin board for the sky and green paper for the ground. Cut out the lettering and attach it to the board.

2. Cut and fold strips of yellow paper according to the instant border directions on page 10. Trace the half-circle border onto the folded paper and cut out. Staple the border around the board's edges.

3. Cut out the wagon and tractor and piece together. Attach the wagon to the board, resting on the green paper, then attach the tractor in front of it.

4. Cut out the hay. Write one of the following on each: true, noble, right, pure, lovely, admirable, excellent and praiseworthy. Stack on the wagon.

5. Cut out the wheels. Cover them with self-stick plastic. Punch holes in the centers of the wheels.

6. Place a paper fastener through each black wheel and the matching side of the green wheel behind it. Spread apart the prongs of the paper fasteners, keeping the top wheel loose enough to turn.

7. Attach the wheels to the board by stapling the green wheels on.

## ✱ Teach

Say, **Do you always think nice thoughts? What kinds of things are nice to think about?** Ask the child to say nice thoughts as they turn the wheels. Remind the children that each time they turn the wheels they should repeat some nice thoughts.

Suggested Usage: Harvest theme

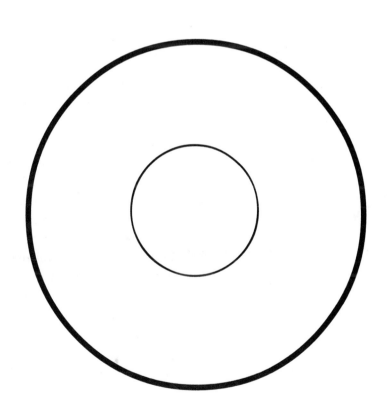

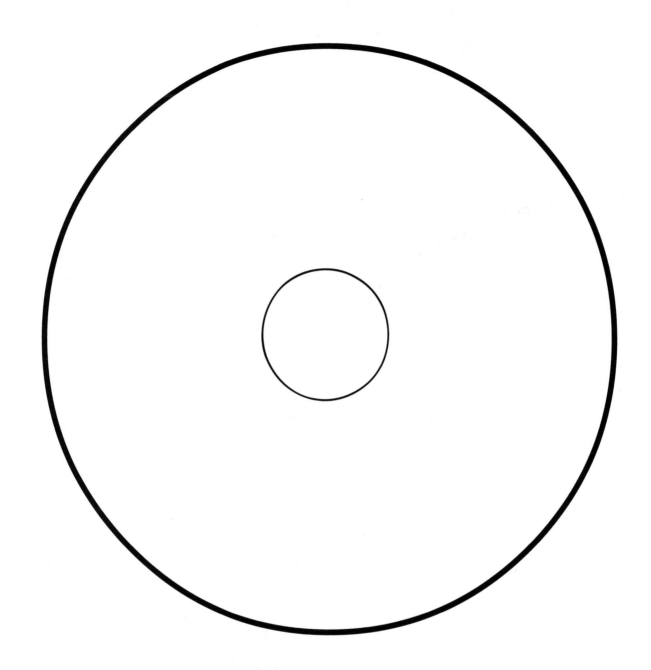

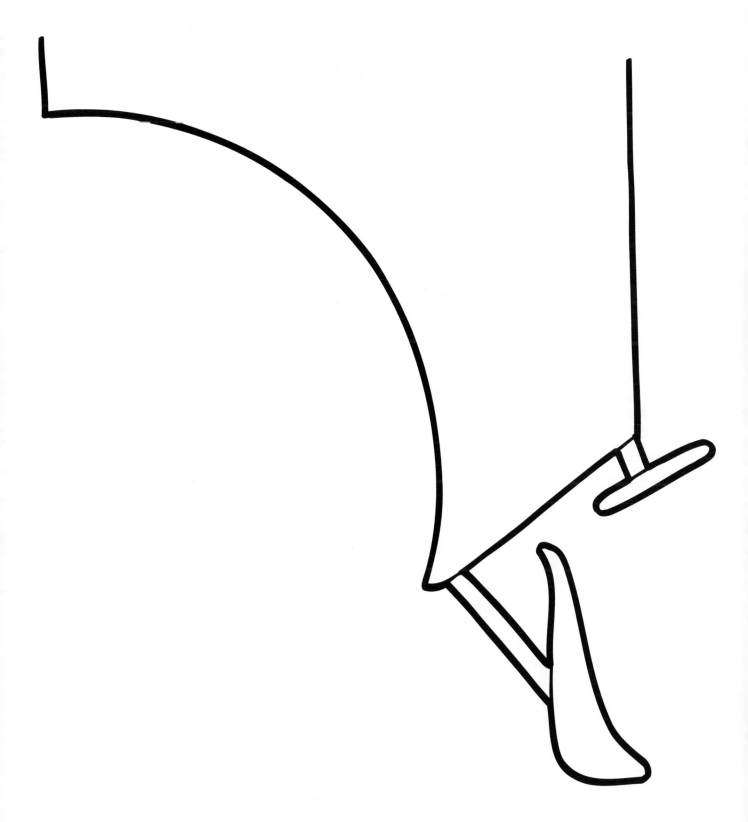

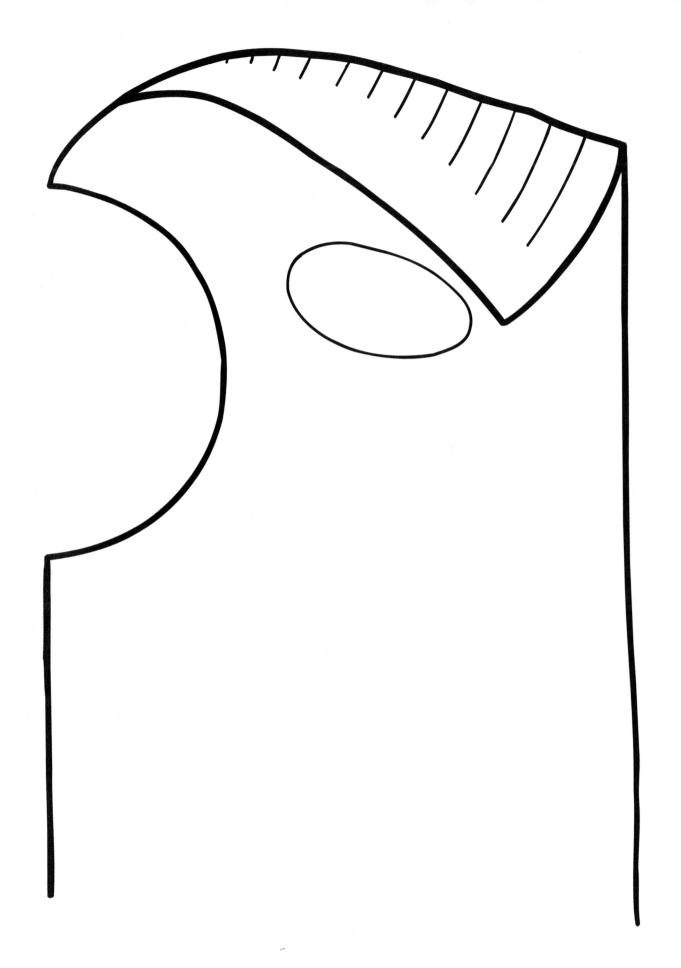

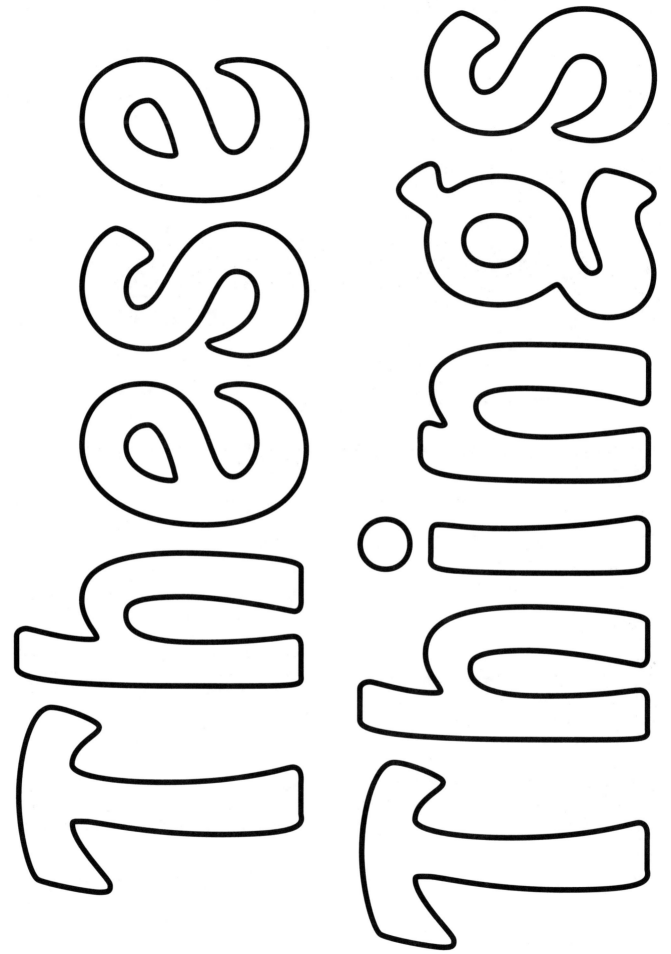

These Things

## Where Is Your Treasure?

**＊ Ages 2-5 ＊**

**＊ Plan**

To emphasize that God should be life's top priority.

**＊ Memorize**

*For where your treasure is, there your heart will be also.* Matthew 6:21

**＊ Gather**

- patterns from pp. 52-57
- pattern for V-shaped border from p. 11
- pattern for lettering from pp. 58-59
- construction paper, orange, brown, yellow and white
- poster paper, blue and green
- glue

**＊ Prepare**

Duplicate two haystacks, the large and small suns and the star on yellow paper; four large pumpkins and one small pumpkin on orange paper; the leaves on green paper; the large and small fences and Jesus on white paper; and the lettering on orange paper.

**＊ Create**

1. Post the blue paper on the bulletin board for the sky and green paper for the ground. Cut out the lettering and attach it to the board.
2. Cut and fold strips of brown paper according to the directions on page 10. Trace the V-shaped border onto the folded paper and cut out. Staple the border around the board's edges.
3. Cut out the haystacks. Make a door on one haystack by cutting upward 3" and to the left 2". Gently fold back the door. Attach both haystacks to the bulletin board. Cut out and glue the small pumpkin behind the door.
4. Cut out three large pumpkins and arrange them in a pumpkin patch. Cut out and glue the small fence on the front of one pumpkin. Cut out the fourth pumpkin and fold it down from the top about ¼". Glue the fold onto the pumpkin with the small fence on it so it flaps open.
5. Cut out the large fence. Cut a door as in #3 on one section. Attach the fence to the board. Glue the small sun picture inside the fence door.
6. Cut out two large suns. Glue the picture of Jesus on one and attach it to the board. Glue the other sun on top of it as in #5.
7. Cut out the small star and glue it on the outside of the haystack with the door.

**＊ Teach**

Ask, **Have you ever been on a treasure hunt? Our verse says that when we find a treasure we find our heart. That means when we love something in our heart we treat it with importance. Let's do the treasure hunt on the bulletin board to find our treasure.** Have the class assist you as you open the haystack, thenthe pumpkin, fence and sun.

Suggested Usage: Harvest theme

51

large fence

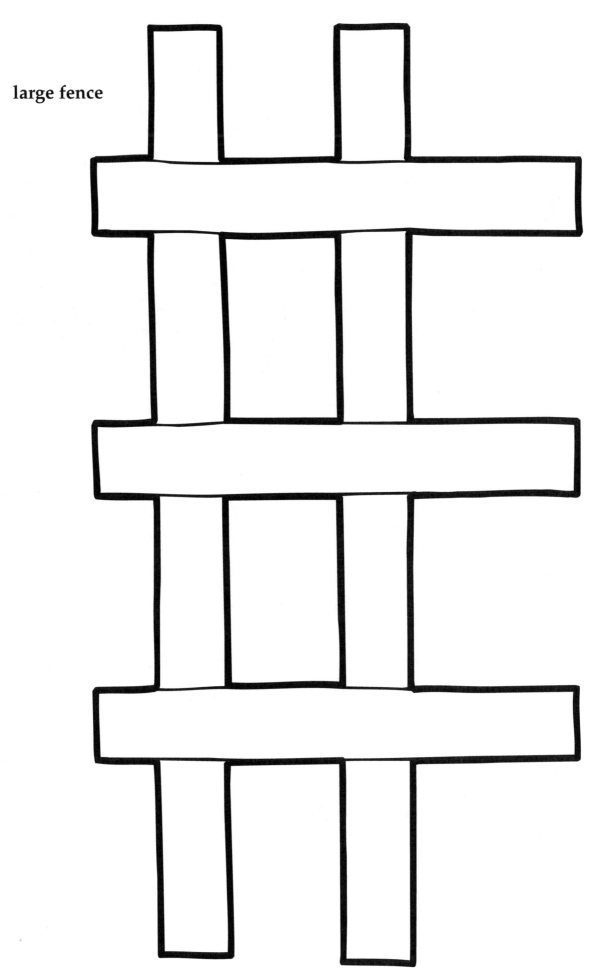

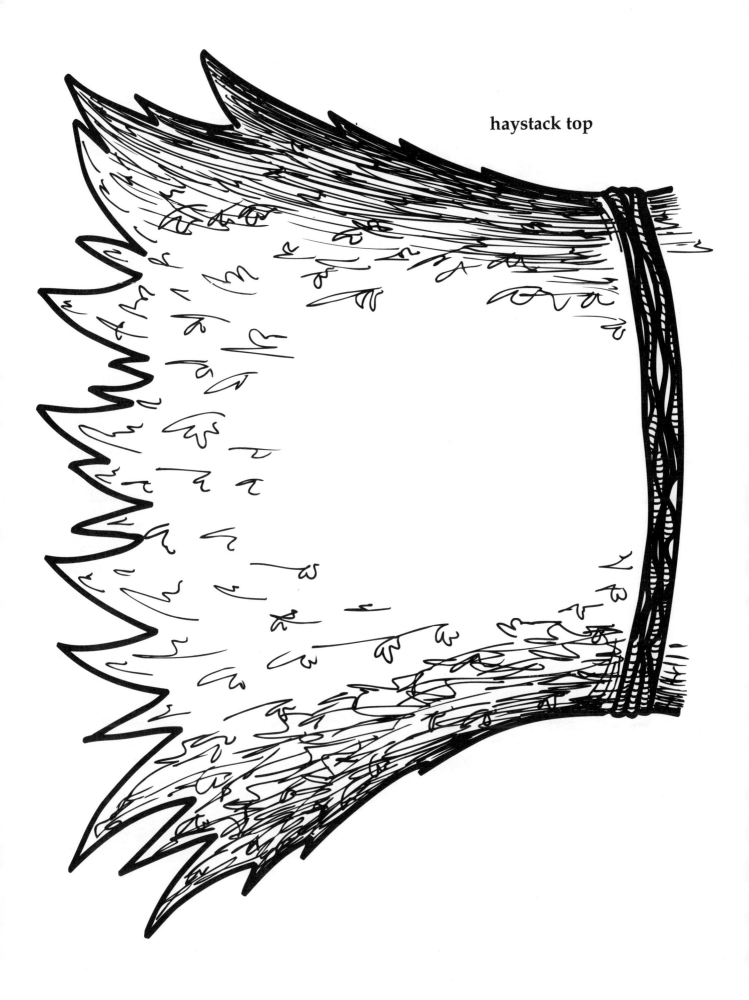

haystack top

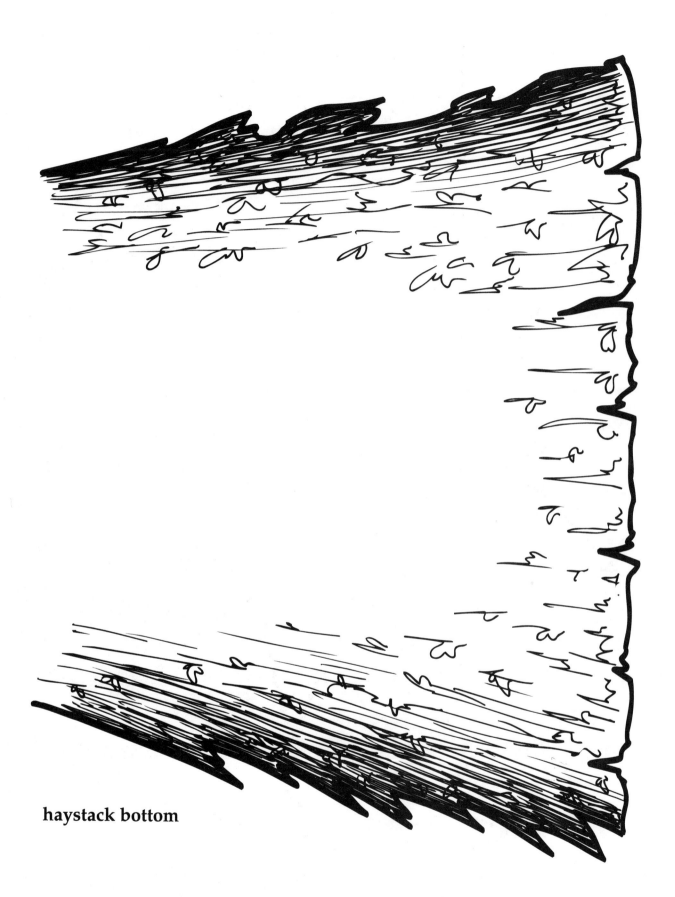

haystack bottom

large sun

small sun

large pumpkin

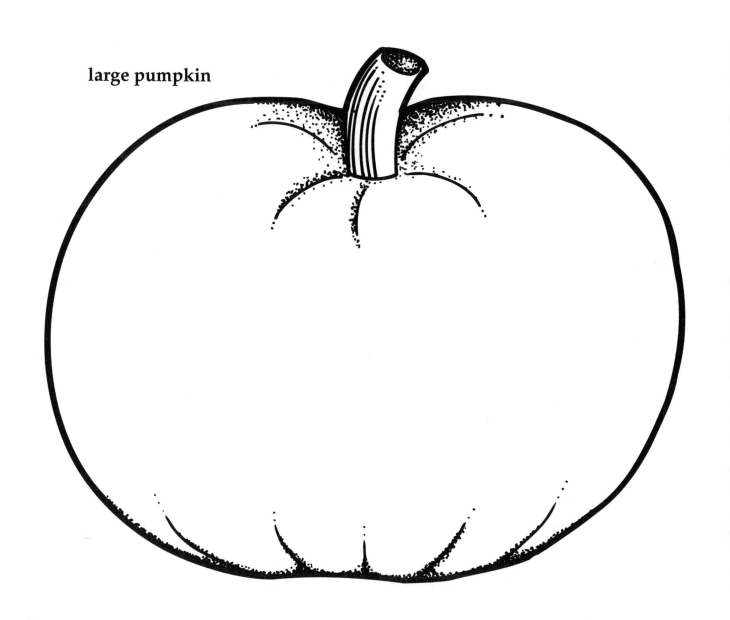

small pumpkin

56

 **star**

**Jesus**

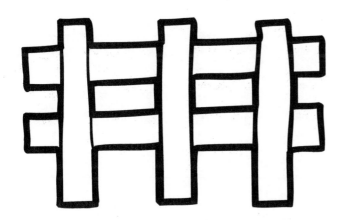 **small fence**

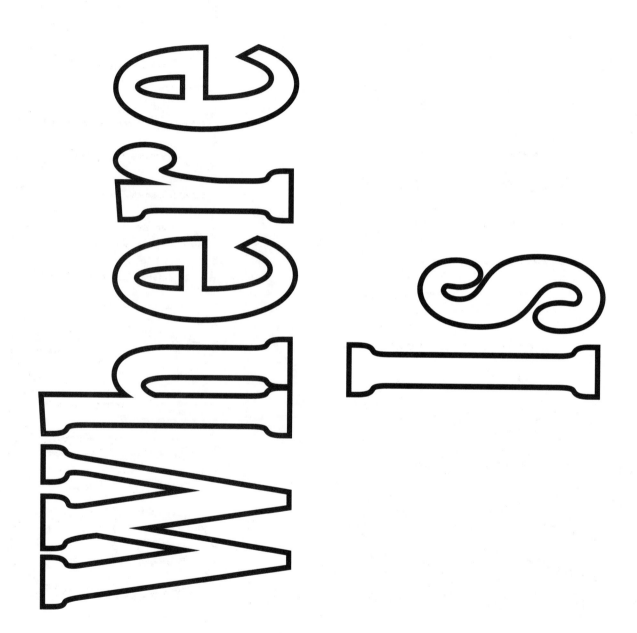

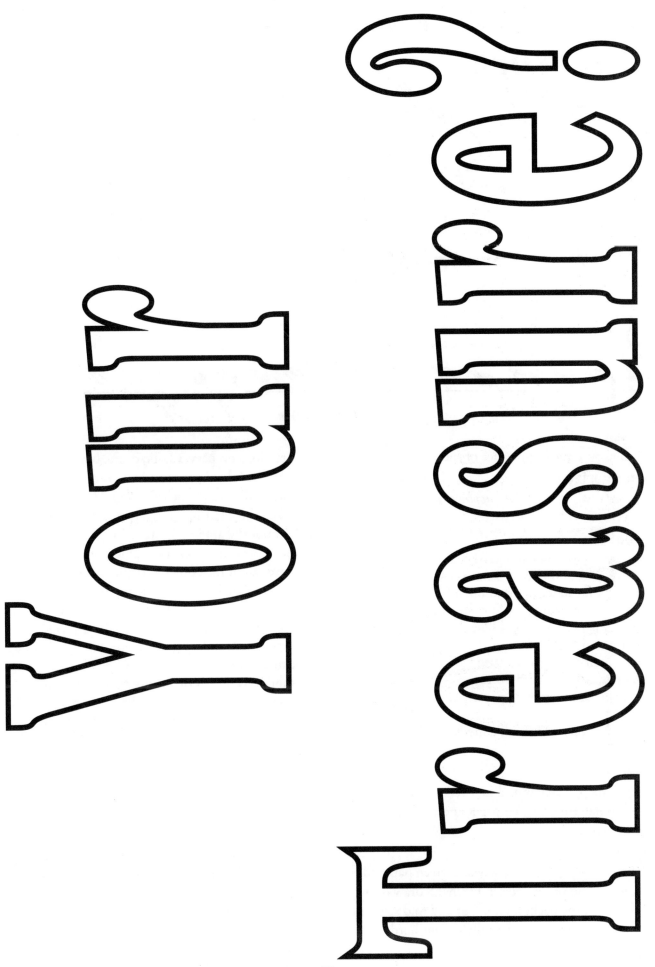

Your Treasure?

**A Word Aptly Spoken Is Like...**

### ✳ Plan
To illustrate the importance of speaking kindly.

### ✳ Memorize
*A word aptly spoken is like apples of gold.*
Proverbs 25:11

### ✳ Gather
- pattern for apple from p. 61
- pattern for leaf border from p. 13
- pattern for lettering from pp. 62-63
- construction paper, yellow, green, red and brown
- poster paper, green and blue
- marker, black
- clear, self-stick plastic
- hole punch
- streamers, green crepe paper
- glue
- utility hooks, nine with adhesive backing
- sliced apples

### ✳ Prepare
Duplicate five yellow and four red apples. Duplicate the leaf pattern on green paper and the lettering on black paper.

### ✳ Create
1. Post blue paper for the sky and green paper for the ground on the board. Freehand draw or paint a tree on the background. Cut and fold strips of green paper according to the instant border directions on page 10. Trace the border pattern onto the folded paper and cut out. Staple the border around the board's edges. Cut out and attach the lettering on the board. Add ellipses.
2. Cut out the apples. Write the memory verse on the apples, one word per apple.
3. Cover all of the apples with clear, self-stick plastic. Punch a hole at the top of each.
4. Cut a tree top from green paper (a cloud shape works well) and attach it to the board. Add texture by wadding green crepe paper and gluing it to the tree.
5. Randomly attach the utility hooks on the tree.
6. Give each child an apple. Have the children help you place them in order on the hooks. As they do so, help them say the words, then say the verse together when you are finished. Remove the apples and repeat to give everyone a turn.

### ✳ Teach
Discuss why Jesus wants us to be kind to others. Ask, **Has anyone ever said anything mean to you about someone else? Do you think Jesus would want you to act that way? Let's make Jesus happy by only talking in nice words.** Follow your lesson with a snack of sliced apples.

*Suggested Usage: Early fall*

60

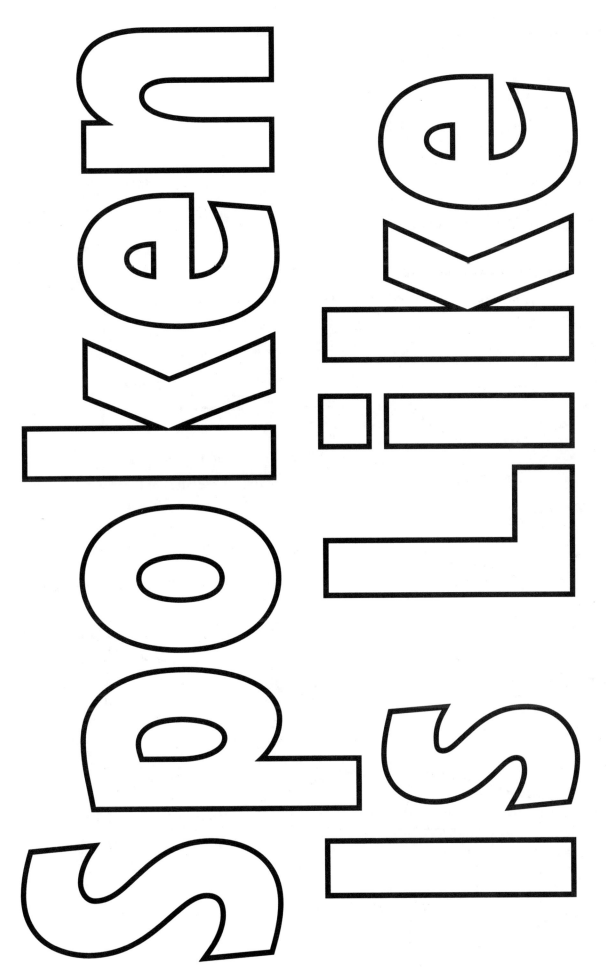

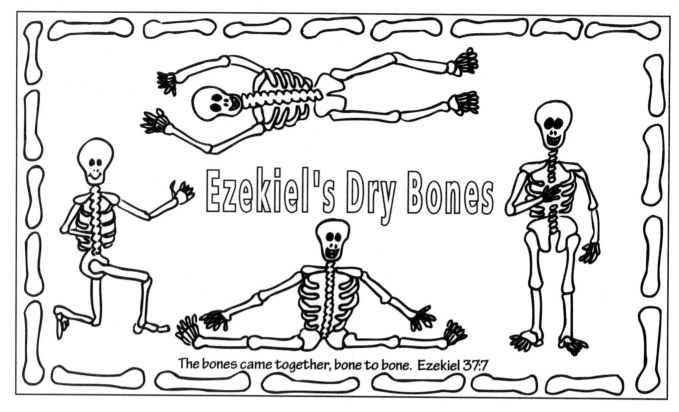

The bones came together, bone to bone. Ezekiel 37:7

## ✳ Plan

To show how God can bring new hope to dead lives.

## ✳ Memorize

*The bones came together, bone to bone.* Ezekiel 37:7

## ✳ Gather

- pattern for lettering from p. 67
- pattern for bones from pp. 65-66
- pattern for bone border from p. 11
- construction paper, white
- background paper, black
- white chalk
- scissors
- paper fasteners

## ✳ Prepare

Duplicate the lettering and the bones patterns (one set for each child) on white construction paper.

## ✳ Create

1. Cover the bulletin board with black background paper. Cut out and attach the lettering to the top center of the board. Use white chalk to write the memory verse at the bottom of the board.
2. Cut and fold strips of white construction paper according to the instant border directions on page 10. Trace the bone border pattern onto the folded paper and cut out the border. Staple the border around the edges of the board.
3. Distribute a set of duplicated bones to each student. Have the students cut out the bones and show how to attach them together using paper fasteners.
4. Allow the students to assist you in positioning and attaching the skeletons to the bulletin board. Write the students' names on the backs of the skeletons so they may take them home after the board is dismantled.

## ✳ Teach

Read the story of Ezekiel's dream from Ezekiel 37:1-14 to the class. Ask, **What did Ezekiel see in the valley?** *Dry bones.* **What can dry bones do?** *Nothing.* **What did God make the dry bones do?** *Come to life.* **What can we learn about God's work in our lives from this story?** *He will help us when we need Him; He gives us new life.*

Suggested Usage: Halloween alternative

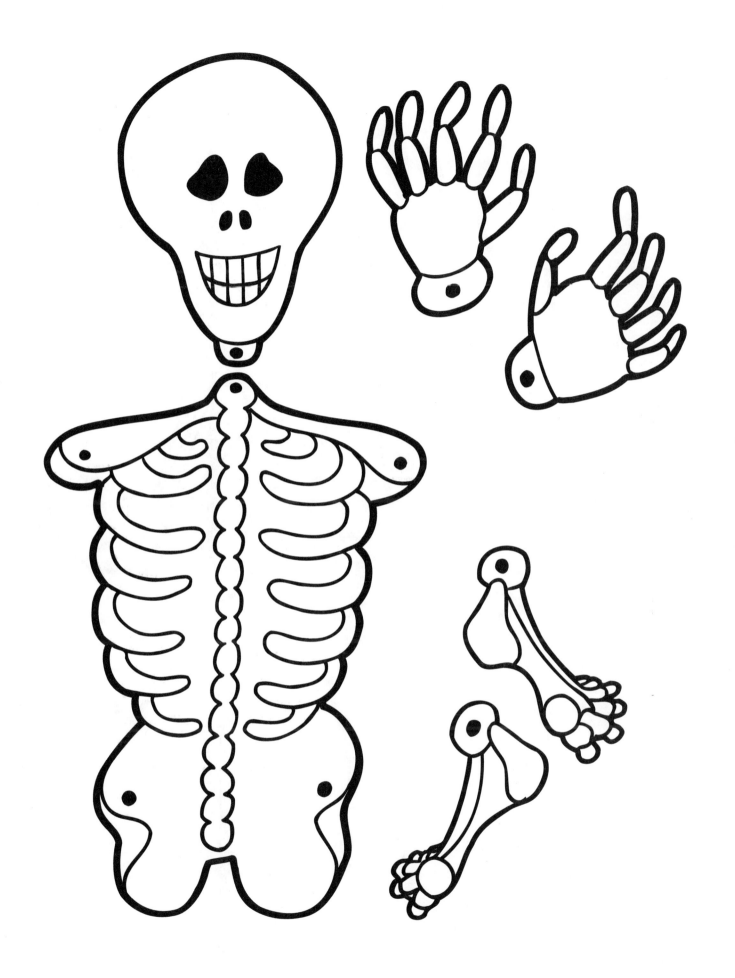

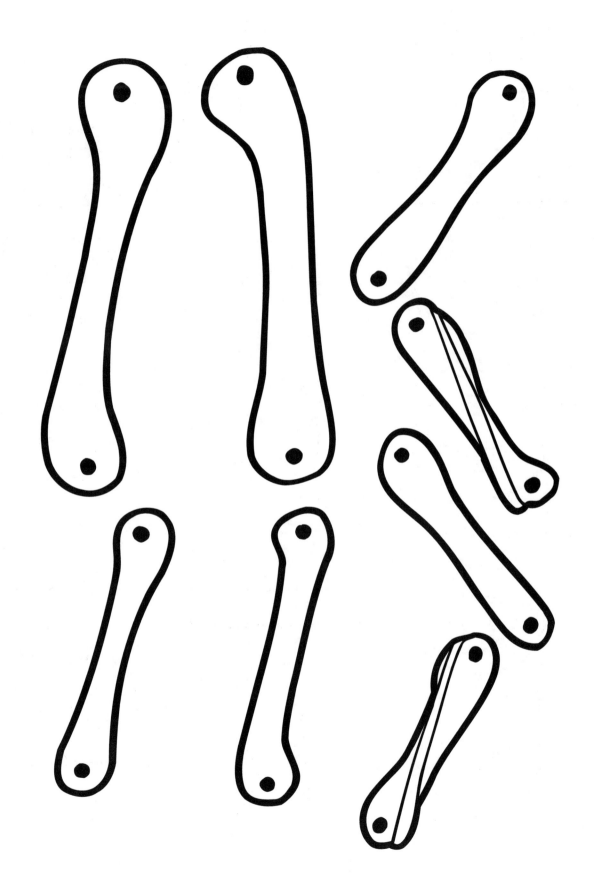

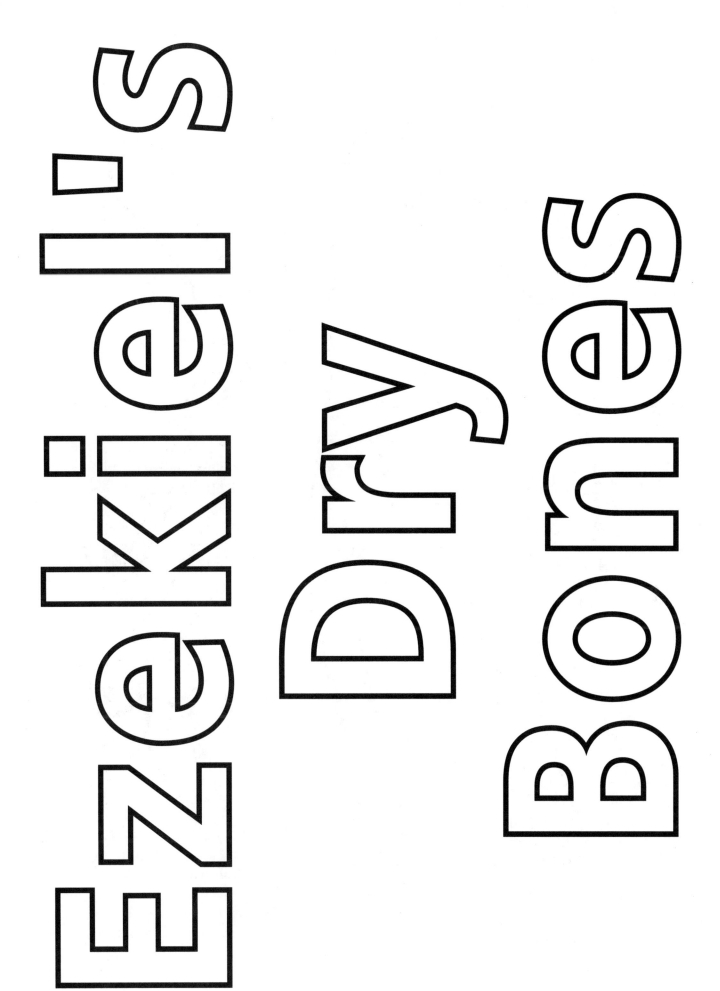

Ezekiel's Dry Bones

# The Light Of Life

## ✳ Plan
To explain how Jesus lights our way.

## ✳ Memorize
*I am the light of the world.* John 8:12

## ✳ Gather
- pattern for lantern from p. 69
- pattern for lettering from pp. 70-71
- pattern for V-shaped border from p. 11
- construction paper, black
- poster paper, blue
- pencil or white crayon
- waxed paper
- crayons
- pencil sharpeners
- electric iron
- glue

## ✳ Prepare
Duplicate the lettering and two lanterns per child on black paper. You will need at least one adult helper with you and the children while the iron is used. Never leave the hot iron unattended.

## ✳ Create
1. Attach the blue paper to the bulletin board. Cut out and post the lettering.
2. Cut and fold strips of black paper according to the instant border directions on page 10. Trace the V-shape border pattern onto the folded paper and cut out. Staple it around the board's edges.
3. Cut out the lanterns. Write the children's names on their lanterns using a pencil or white crayon.
4. Give each child a piece of waxed paper. Show how to make shavings onto the waxed paper with a crayon and pencil sharpener. Emphasize the importance of using several colors of crayons.
5. Place another piece of waxed paper over the shavings. Using low heat, gently iron the waxed paper packet until the shavings melt.
6. Show how to position the waxed paper between the lantern pieces and glue around the edges. After the glue dries, have the students assist you as you attach the lanterns to the bulletin board.

## ✳ Teach
Ask, **What happens when we turn off a light or when the sun goes down at night? What happens when we turn on a light or burn a candle, or when the sun comes up? Jesus says He is the Light of the world. That means He came to show us the way to live, just like a light makes it easier to see where we are going. If we follow Him, we will always be able to see where we should go.**

Suggested Usage: Halloween alternative (light vs. dark)

The Light

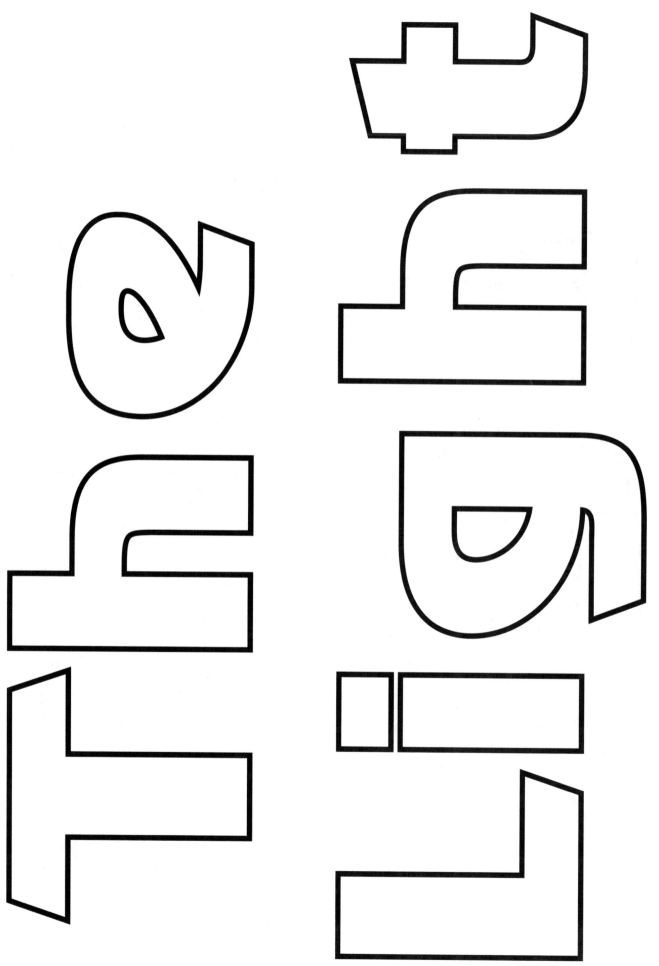

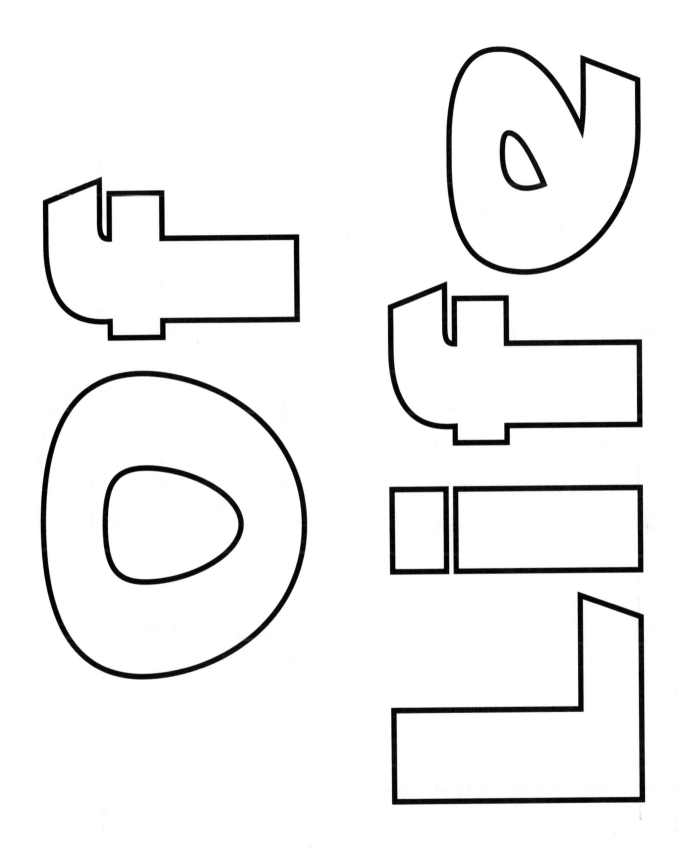

# Pumpkin Seeds Of Faith

*The seed on good soil produce[s] a crop. Luke 8:15*

### ✱ Ages 6-10 ✱

## ✱ Plan
To learn that God honors those who follow Him.

## ✱ Memorize
*The seed on good soil produce[s] a crop.* Luke 8:15

## ✱ Gather
- poster paper, green or yellow
- pattern for lettering from pp. 75-76
- pattern for pumpkin and seed from pp. 73-74
- pattern for pumpkin border from p. 12
- construction paper, orange and brown
- drawing paper, manila
- marker, black
- clear, self-stick plastic
- plastic sandwich bag
- push pin

## ✱ Prepare
Duplicate the lettering on brown paper. Duplicate eight pumpkins on orange paper and eight seeds on manila drawing paper.

## ✱ Create
1. Cover the board with green or yellow paper. Cut out the lettering and attach it. Write the memory verse at the bottom of the board.
2. Cut and fold strips of orange paper according to the instant border directions on page 10. Trace the border onto the folded paper and cut out. Staple the border around the board's edges.
3. Cut out the pumpkins and seeds. Cut a slit in each pumpkin at the center line.
4. On each pumpkin, use a black marker to write one of the "Who Am I?" questions from p. 73.
5. Write one of the Bible character name answers from p. 73 on the front of each seed and the correct question number on the seed's back.
6. Cover the pumpkins and seeds with self-stick plastic for durability.
7. Staple the pumpkins to the board, leaving the slits open. Pin a plastic sandwich bag on the board for storing the seeds when not in use.
8. Invite the students to match the seeds with the correct pumpkins by sliding the seed into the pumpkin's slit. They may check their answers by turning the seeds over.

## ✱ Teach
Reverse the game by selecting a seed, reading the name to the class, and asking, **What did this person do to honor God?** Students may answer from the prepared questions on the bulletin board or they may offer their own answers. After the game, ask, **Why should we listen to God and do what He says? What can we do to honor God in our lives?**

Suggested Usage: Harvest/Halloween alternative

# "Who Am I" questions for Pumpkin Seeds of Faith

1. I built an ark because I believed God would send a great rain. Who am I?

2. I led the Israelites into the wilderness because I believed God would lead us to the Promised Land. Who am I?

3. I believed God would make my descendants as numerous as the stars in heaven. Who am I?

4. I had faith that God would deliver me from the lions' den. Who am I?

5. I gave my life to the sharing of the gospel because I believed it to be true. Who am I?

6. I believed God would help me crumble the walls of Jericho. Who am I?

7. I knew God would help me defeat the giant Goliath. Who am I?

8. Because of my faith, I was chosen to be the mother of Jesus. Who am I?

**Answers**

Noah (1), Moses (2), Abraham (3), Daniel (4), Paul (5), Joshua (6), David (7) and Mary (8)

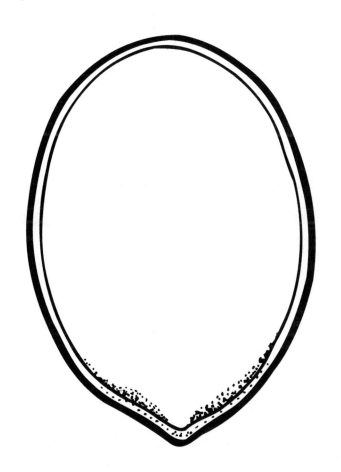

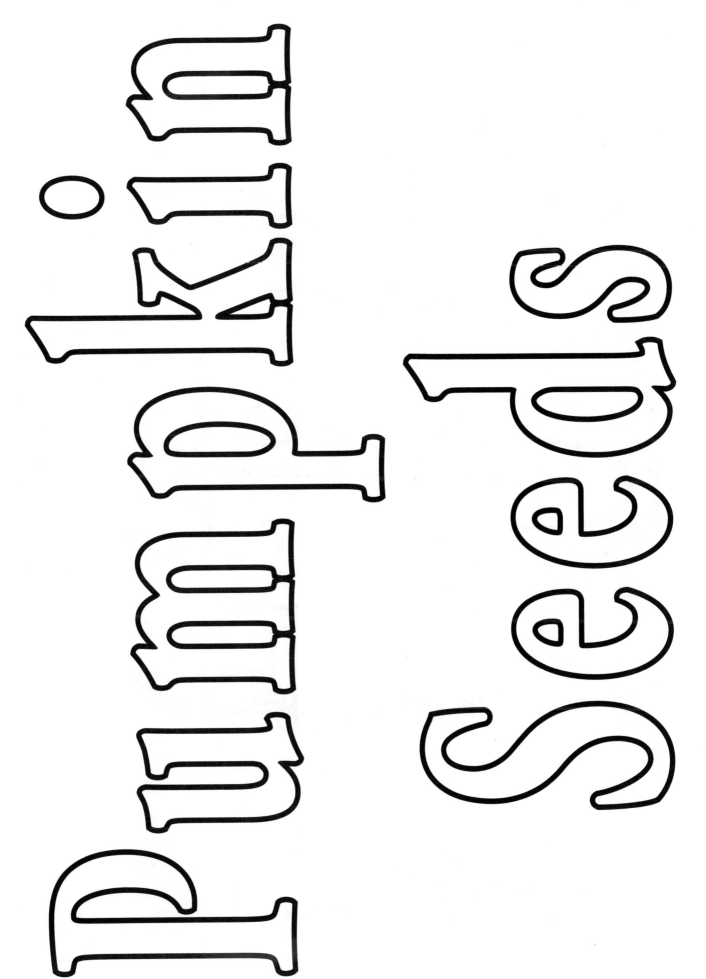

Pumpkin Seeds

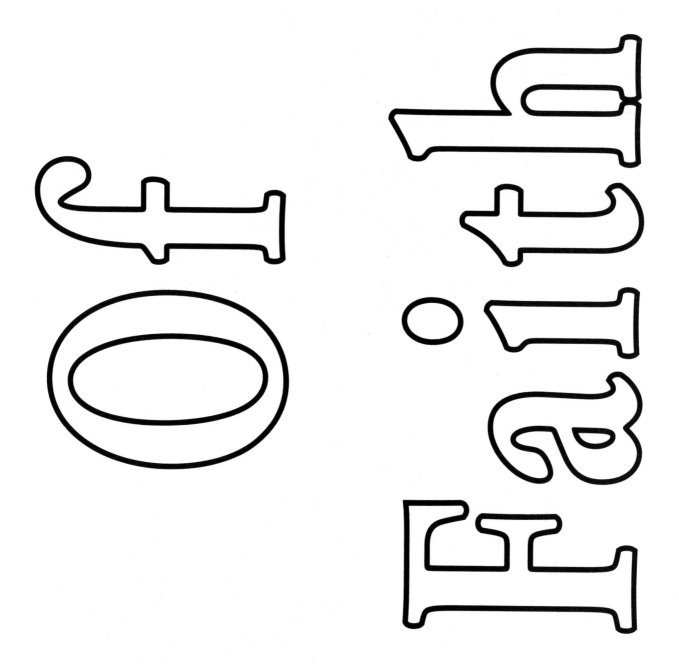

## ✻ Plan
To identify God-given skills and His command to use them to His glory.

## ✻ Memorize
*Do you see a man skilled in his work? He will serve before kings.* Proverbs 22:29

## ✻ Gather
- pattern for spider from p. 78
- pattern for lettering from pp. 79-80
- pattern for V-shaped border from p. 11
- construction paper, black
- poster paper, yellow
- yarn, one skein of black or gray
- paper clips
- masking tape
- crayon, white

## ✻ Prepare
Trace and cut out the lettering from black paper and one spider for each child from white paper.

## ✻ Create
1. Post the yellow paper on the board. Cut out and attach the lettering.
2. Cut and fold strips of black paper according to the instant border directions on page 10. Trace the V-shaped border pattern onto the folded paper and cut out. Staple the border around the board's edges.
3. Create a spider web with the yarn by stapling one end to the bottom of the board and weaving it up, down and across the board. Staple the yarn before changing directions, at least every 12".
4. Open one end of a paper clip by bending the center upward like a hook. Secure one end of the clip to the back of the spider with masking tape.
5. Write each child's name on a spider with a white crayon.

## ✻ Teach
Say, **What is this on the bulletin board? A spider's web! Have you ever seen a real spider's web? What did it look like? Did you know that a spider works very hard to create a web? When God created spiders, He gave them the ability to spin webs to catch their food. God also gives us the ability to do good things—we call them "skills." What kinds of skills do you have? God says if you use your skills and work hard, He will be happy with you. Let's all work hard at our skills and make God happy.** After the discussion, give the children their spiders and allow them to place them on the web as they name a skill God gave them. The spiders will slide from staple to staple on the web.

Suggested Usage: Halloween alternative

77

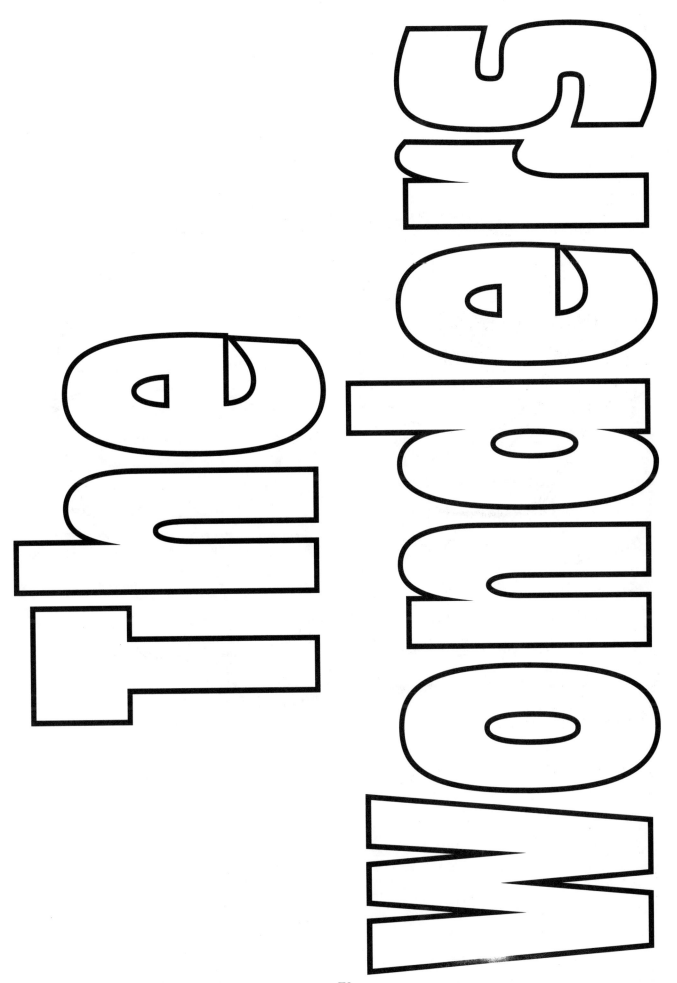

The Wonders

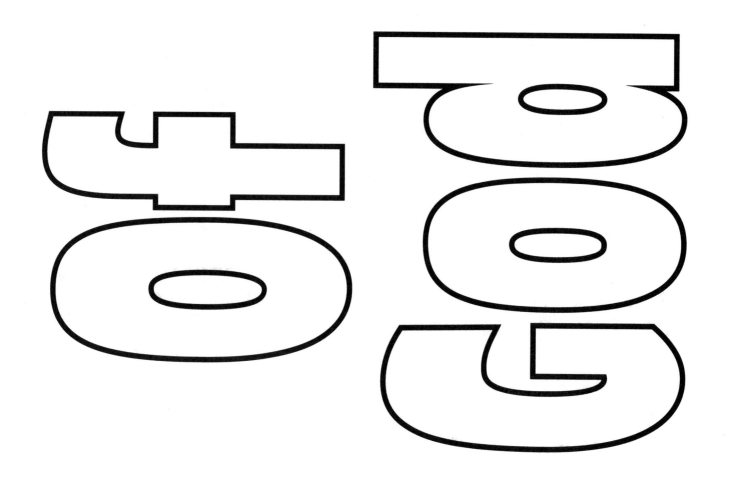

## ✳ Plan

To recognize the ways in which God blesses us.

## ✳ Memorize

*Give thanks to the Lord.* 1 Chronicles 16:8

## ✳ Gather

- patterns for turkey from pp. 82-84
- pattern for hand border from p. 12
- pattern for lettering from pp. 85-86
- construction paper, brown, yellow, red and orange
- poster paper, yellow
- pencils
- safety scissors
- marker, black
- crayons

## ✳ Prepare

Duplicate the turkey on white paper and color in. Duplicate the lettering on red paper.

## ✳ Create

1. Attach the yellow background paper to the board. Cut out the lettering and post.
2. Cut and fold strips of construction paper according to the instant border directions on page 10. Trace the hand border pattern onto the folded paper and cut out the border. Staple the border around the edges of the board.
3. Cut out the turkey body and attach it to the middle of the board.
4. Allow each child to select a sheet of construction paper. Help them trace their hands on the paper. Then allow them to the cut out their traced hands and help them write their names on them.
5. Position and staple the hands on each side of the turkey to represent its feathers. Attach the turkey's head on top of the body and feathers.

## ✳ Teach

Say, **What are we supposed to say when someone does something nice for us?** *Thank you.* **God likes for us to tell Him when we are thankful, too. Even though He knows everything about us, it is still important for us to talk to Him about our blessings. Let's name some things for which we are thankful and I will write them on your turkey "feather" so everyone will know how good God has been to you.** Allow the children to individually name things for their feathers as you write them.

Suggested Usage: Thanksgiving

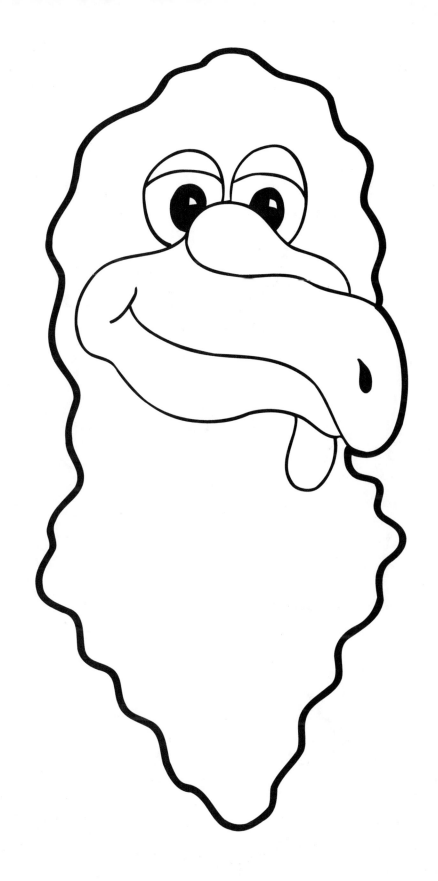

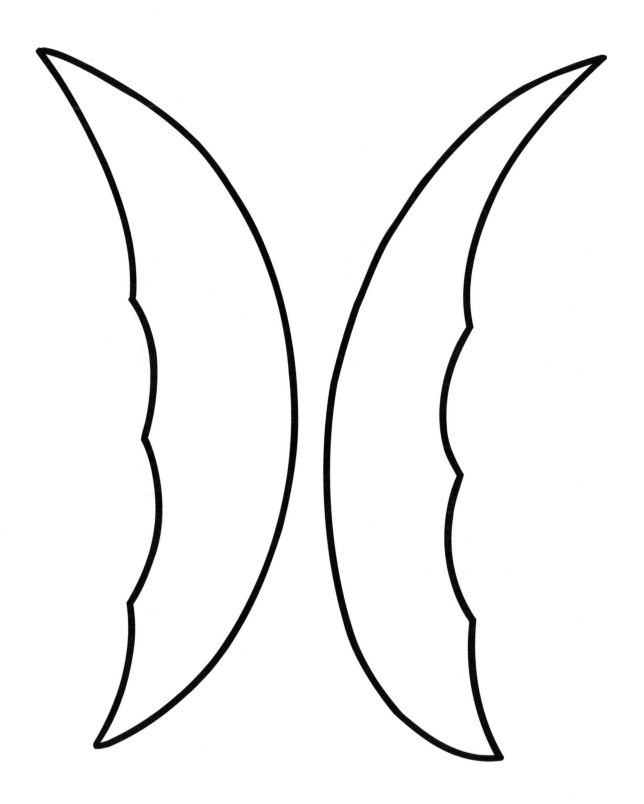

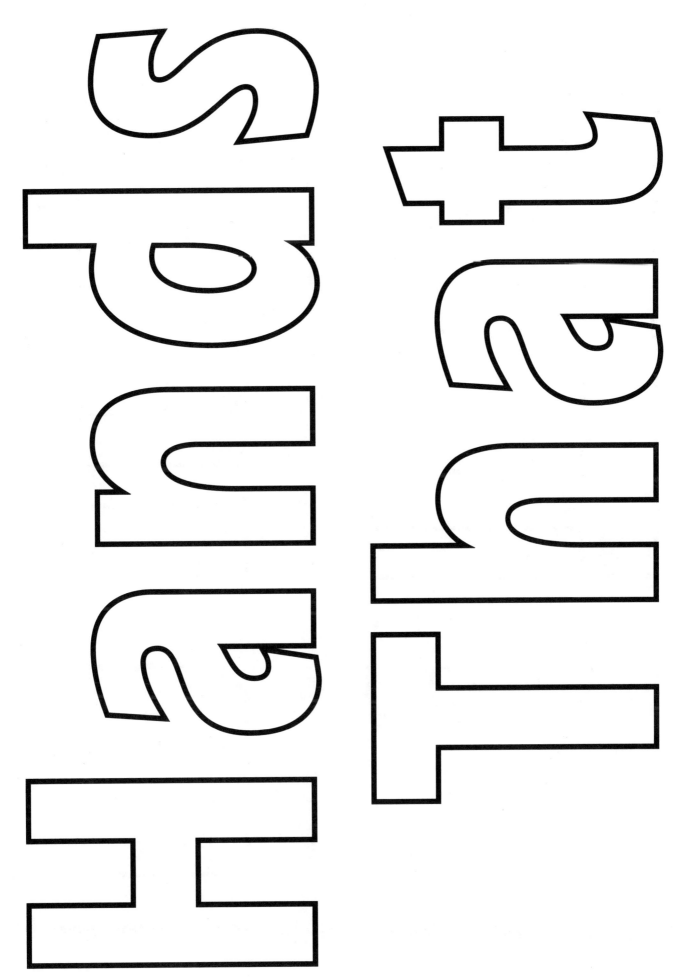

Hands

That

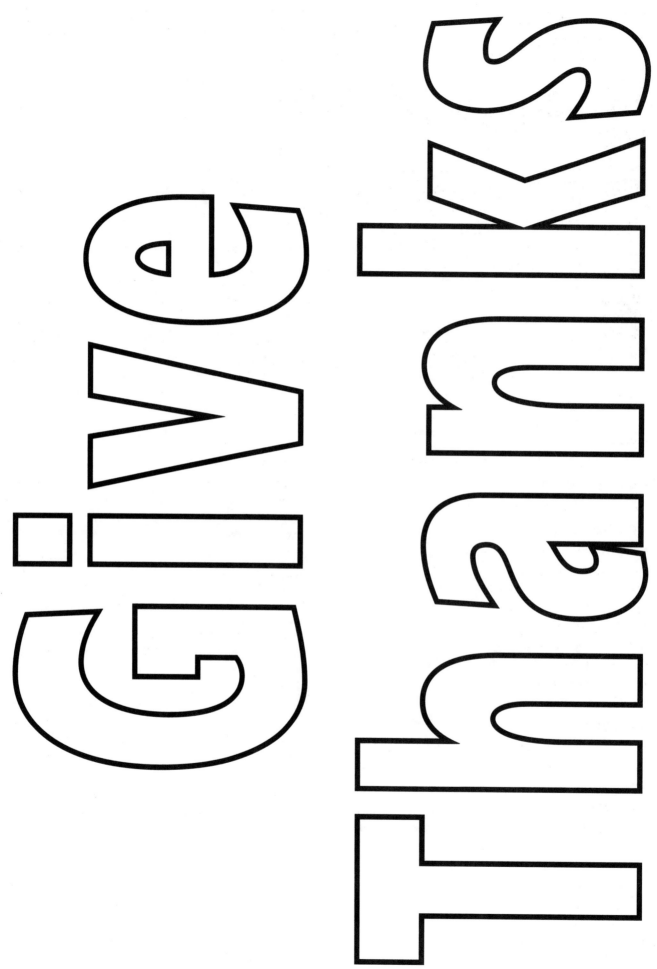

## ✷ Plan

To learn that thanking God is important.

## ✷ Memorize

*One of them came back, praising God.* Luke 17:15

## ✷ Gather

- pattern for figures from pp. 88-90
- pattern for lettering from pp. 91-92
- pattern for hand border from p. 12
- construction paper, various colors
- background paper, yellow
- crayons, markers, or colored pencils
- marker, black
- clear, self-stick plastic
- Velcro

## ✷ Prepare

Duplicate nine standing men, one kneeling man and Jesus on white paper, and the lettering on black paper.

## ✷ Create

1. Attach the yellow paper to the board. Cut out and post the lettering.
2. Cut and fold strips of paper according to the instant border directions on page 10. Trace the hand border onto the folded paper and cut out. Staple the border around the board's edges.
3. Cut out the nine standing men, the kneeling man and Jesus. Allow the students to color the figures (assign figures to pairs if you have a large class).
4. Number the standing men from 2 through 10 by writing the numbers on the fronts of their robes. Write number 1 on the kneeling man.
5. Laminate the figures with clear, self-stick plastic for durability. Place a piece of Velcro on the back of each figure and on the corresponding position on the board. All of the figures should be in a straight line, starting with Jesus on the right, then the kneeling man to the left and the other nine to his left.
6. Allow the children to take the men off of the board and replace them in the correct order.

## ✷ Teach

Read the story of the ten lepers to the class from Luke 17:11-19 or from a Bible story book. Then ask, **Do you sometimes forget to say thank-you like the lepers in this story did? It is important to God that we remember to thank Him for all of the wonderful things He does for us.** Then have the students remove the numbered men from the bulletin board and name something for which they are thankful as they place the men back on the board.

Suggested Usage: Thanksgiving

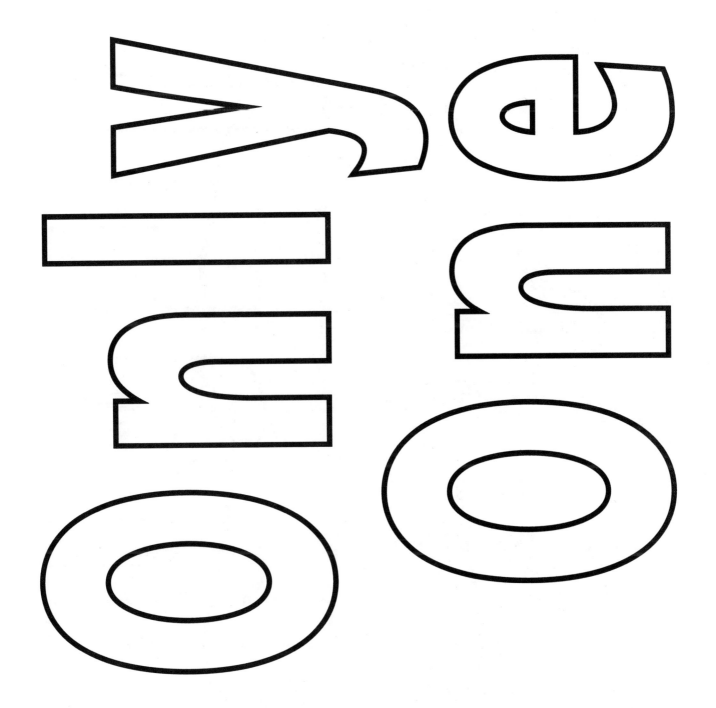

**Give thanks to him.  Psalm 100:4**

* Ages 6-10 *

## * Plan
To identify things for which we are thankful.

## * Memorize
*Give thanks to him.*  Psalm 100:4

## * Gather
- poster paper, yellow
- pattern for lettering from p. 96
- pattern for turkey and feathers from pp. 94-95
- pattern for feather border from p. 12
- construction paper, black, brown and assorted colors
- markers
- glue

## * Prepare
Duplicate the lettering on black construction paper. Duplicate one turkey per child on brown construction paper and several feathers per child on colored paper.

## * Create
1. Cover the bulletin board with yellow background paper. Cut out the lettering and attach it to the bulletin board in the top center. Use a black marker to write the memory verse at the bottom of the board.

2. Cut and fold strips of brown and orange paper according to the instant border directions on page 10. Trace the feather border pattern onto the folded paper and cut out the border. Staple the border around the board's edges.
3. Have the students cut out the turkey and the feathers. Ask the children to write their names on the front of each turkey.
4. On each feather, have them write something for which they are grateful to God. Show how to glue the feathers to the back of each turkey.
5. Attach the turkeys to the bulletin board.

## * Teach
Say, When someone does something nice for you, do you say, "Thank you"? What about if you do something nice for others—do they thank you? How do you feel when you do something nice and the other person shows appreciation? It makes us feel good. That's why we should always give thanks to God. He does so many nice things for us that we should constantly be thanking and praising Him. For the rest of the day, try to remember to say silent prayers of thanks to God for everything you appreciate.

Suggested Usage: Thanksgiving

93

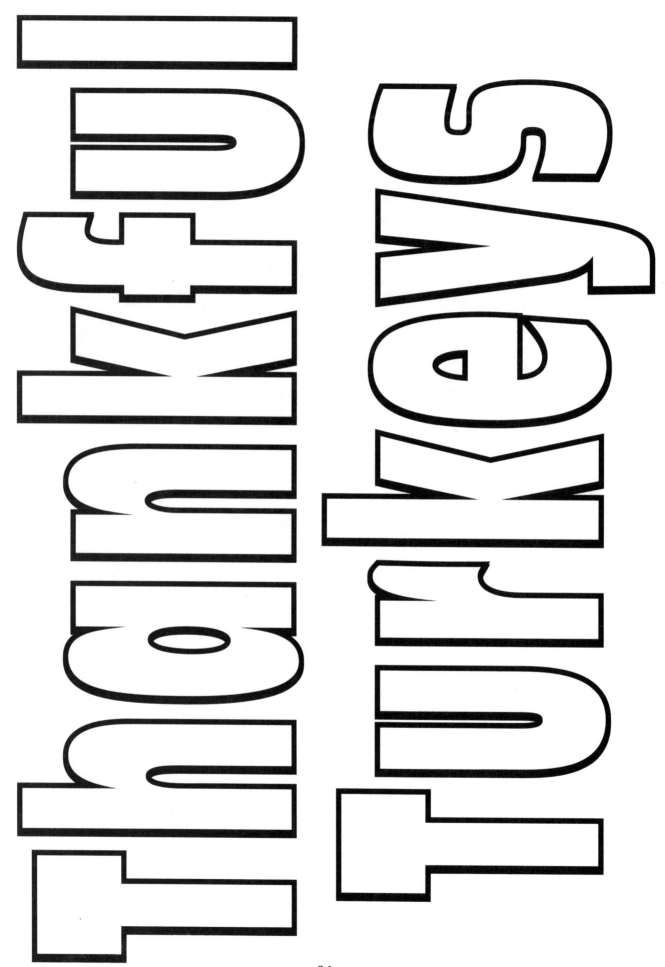

Thankful Turkeys

Done Any Good Deeds Lately?

wash dishes

set the table

sweep floor

pick up toys

clean my room

walk the dog

mow the yard

Let us consider how we may spur one another on toward love and good deeds. Hebrews 10:24

✳ **Ages 6-10** ✳

## ✳ Plan

To emphasize the importance of acting like Christ toward others.

## ✳ Memorize

*Let us consider how we may spur one another on toward love and good deeds.* Hebrews 10:24

## ✳ Gather

- pattern for lettering from pp. 99-100
- patterns for boot and spur from p. 98
- white paper
- poster paper, dark blue
- bandannas
- iron-on interfacing
- rope
- straight pins
- aluminum foil
- glue
- crayons
- safety scissors

## ✳ Prepare

Duplicate the cowboy boot and spur patterns on white paper, one set for each child.

## ✳ Create

1. Cover the bulletin board with dark blue paper.
2. Following the iron-on interfacing's package directions, iron the interfacing to the back sides of the bandannas. Use the letter patterns to trace and cut out letters from the bandanna and attach them to the center of the board.
3. Use a black marker to write the memory verse at the bottom of the board. For a border, use pins to secure a rope around the board's edges.
4. Distribute a duplicated cowboy boot to each student. Have the students color and cut out the boots.
5. Pass out the duplicated spurs and pieces of aluminum foil. Have the children cut out and trace the spur onto foil, then glue the spur to the boot.
6. Ask the students to write on their boots a good deed that a Christian should perform.
7. Attach the boots to the board.

## ✳ Teach

Use a Western theme for your class the day this bulletin board is constructed. Some ideas: dress in Western clothing, "brand" the children as they enter the class with a carved potato stamped onto an ink pad, play Christian country music, collect your class offering in a cowboy boot, or serve a snack of biscuits on tin plates. End the session with a prayer that the students will be able to share Christ by performing their good deeds.

Suggested Usage: Western theme day

97

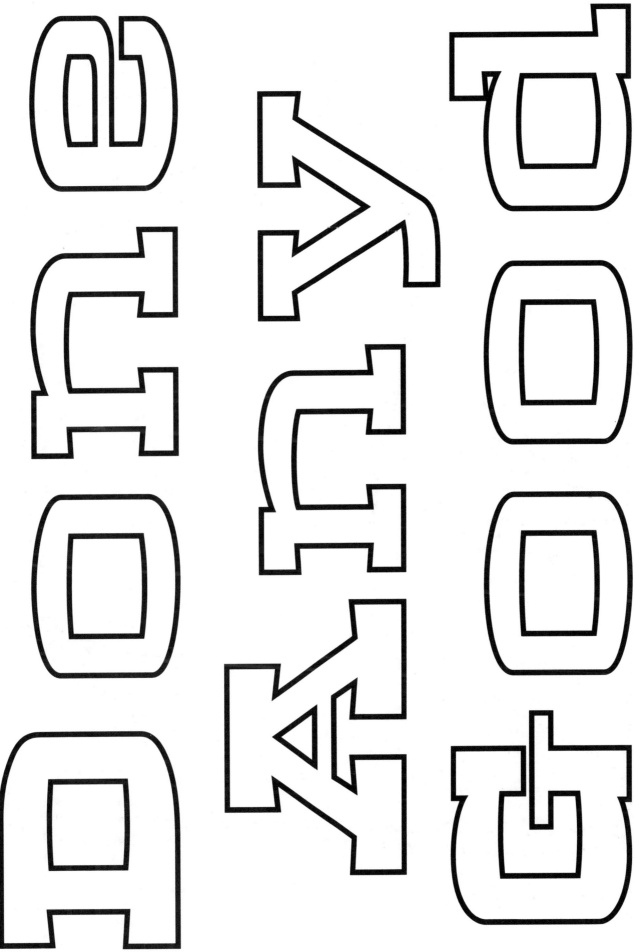

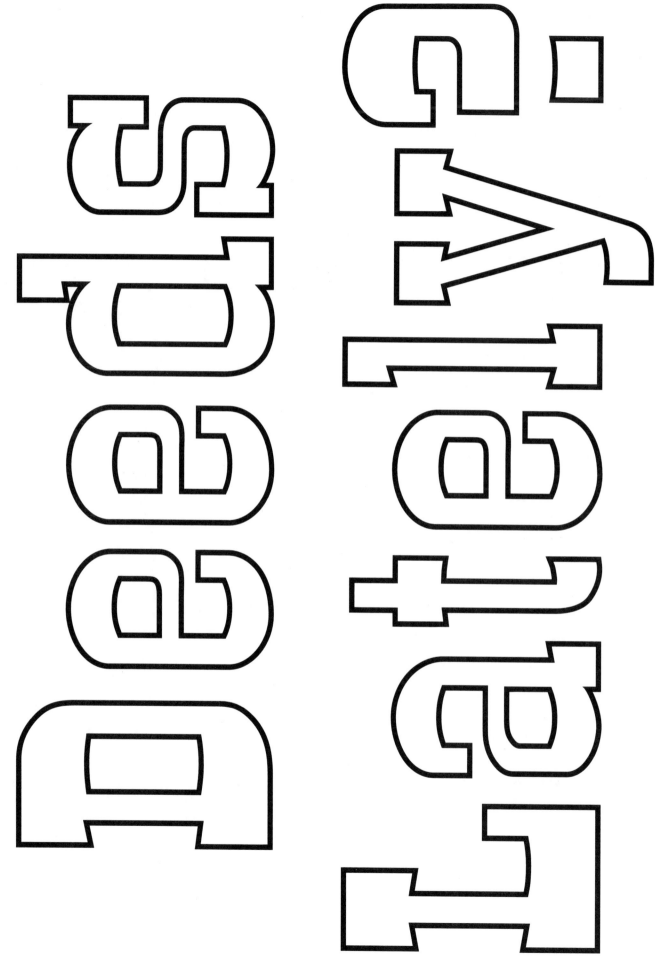

How beautiful are the feet of those who bring good news. Isaiah 52:7

**✳ Ages 6-10 ✳**

### ✳ Plan
To stress individual ability to share the Good News.

### ✳ Memorize
*How beautiful are the feet of those who bring good news.* Isaiah 52:7

### ✳ Gather
- pattern for lettering from p. 103
- pattern for V-shaped border from p. 11
- pattern for newspaper from p. 102
- construction paper, black and white
- newspaper, old
- marker, black
- crayons

### ✳ Prepare
Duplicate the lettering on black construction paper and the front-page pattern on white paper.

### ✳ Create
1. Cover the bulletin board with the white background paper. Cut out the lettering and attach it to the board. Use a black marker to write the memory verse at the bottom of the board.
2. Cut and fold strips of newspaper according to the instant border directions on page 10. Trace the V-shaped border pattern onto the folded paper and cut out the border. Attach the border to the edges of the board.
3. Explain to the class that the word *gospel* means "good news." Distribute a front-page to each student. Ask them to pretend they are writing a newspaper to share the Good News of the gospel with others. Ask, **What could you write? What would the headline be? What pictures could you draw?** Have them use crayons to fill in the front-page.
4. Attach the front-pages to the bulletin board.

### ✳ Teach
Distribute the old newspapers again and ask the students to individually look for something in the newspapers that needs their prayers. Younger children with limited reading ability can look at the newspaper photos. Have each child explain why he or she chose the story and how God can help the situation. Then lead the class in prayer for each need, emphasizing the importance of sharing the Good News.

Suggested Usage: General

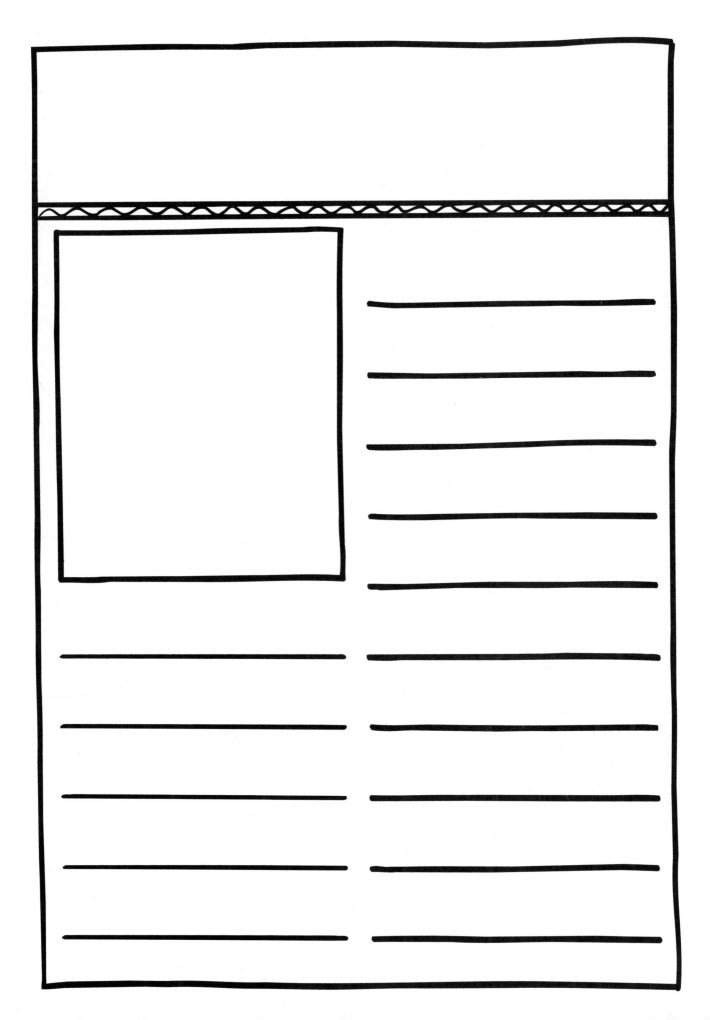

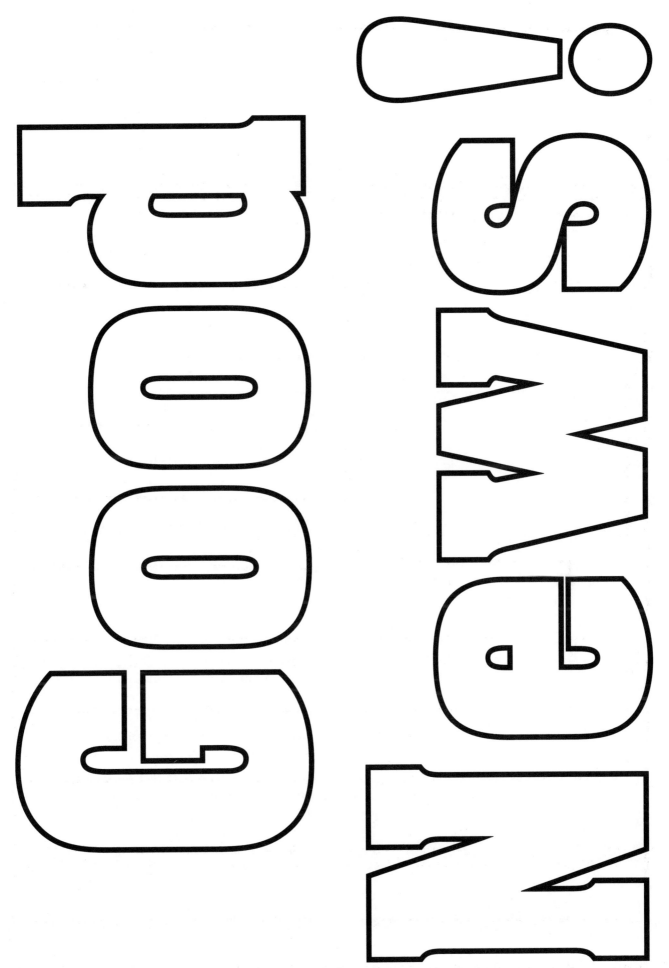

There is a time for everything. Ecclesiastes 3:1

## ✳ Ages 6-10 ✳

### ✳ Plan

To understand that God has a plan for life.

### ✳ Memorize

*There is a time for everything.* Ecclesiastes 3:1

### ✳ Gather

• pattern for lettering from p. 106
• pattern for semi-circle border from p. 11
• pattern for clock face and hands from p. 105
• construction paper, black
• poster paper, yellow
• paper, white
• black marker
• paper plates
• paper fasteners
• crayons
• safety scissors
• glue

### ✳ Prepare

Duplicate the lettering on black construction paper, and the clock face pattern on white paper.

### ✳ Create

1. Cover the bulletin board with yellow paper. Cut out the lettering and attach it to the board. Write the memory verse at the bottom of the board with black marker.
2. Cut and fold strips of black construction paper according to the instant border directions on page

10. Trace the semi-circle border pattern onto the folded paper and cut out the border. Staple the border around the edges of the board.

3. Distribute paper plates, paper fasteners and clock face patterns to the students. Have them use scissors and crayons to color and cut out the clock faces. Show how to glue the clock faces to the center of the paper plate and how to attach the clock hands to the plate with a paper fastener.
4. Attach the clocks to the board.

### ✳ Teach

Play some time-oriented games, such as relays or pencil puzzles. Then ask the class, **As we were playing the game, did you find yourself looking at the clock or wondering how much time was left? That was fun, wasn't it? But sometimes we get too caught up in worrying about the time, especially when we want God to do something for us. He tells us in our memory verse that He is in control of the time in our lives, even if we do not always feel like He is in control. So the next time we are worried about God helping us, we should remember that He is always there watching over us and seeing that everything in our lives happens for a reason, if we look to Him for guidance.**

Suggested Usage: General

104

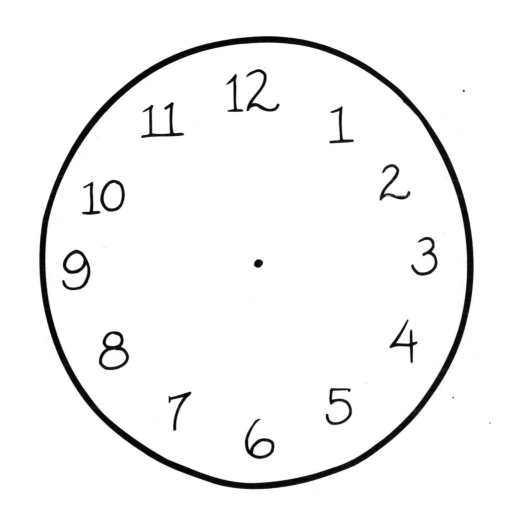

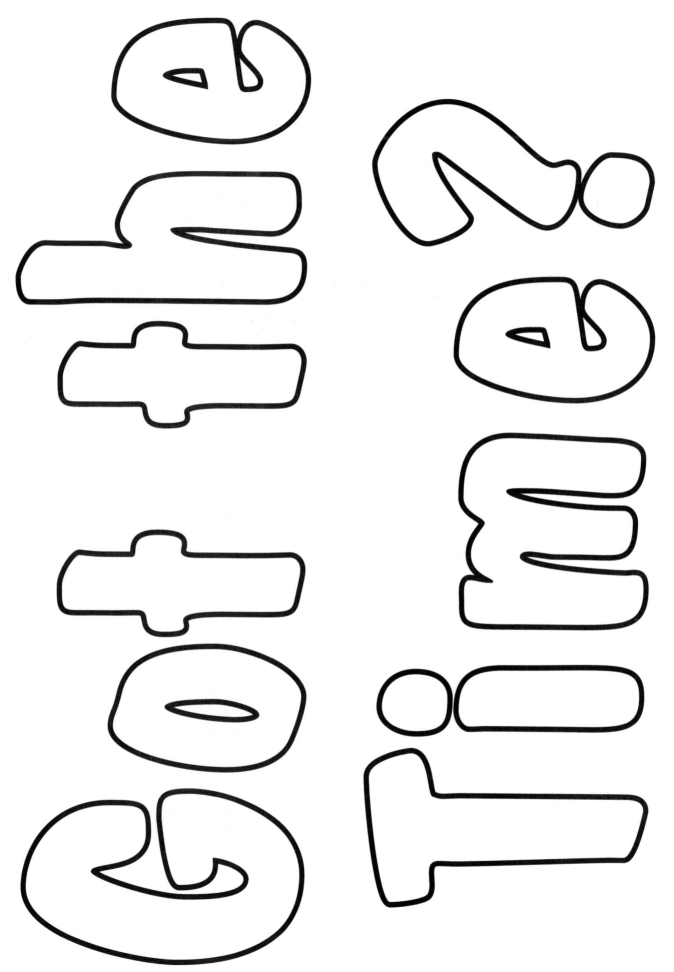

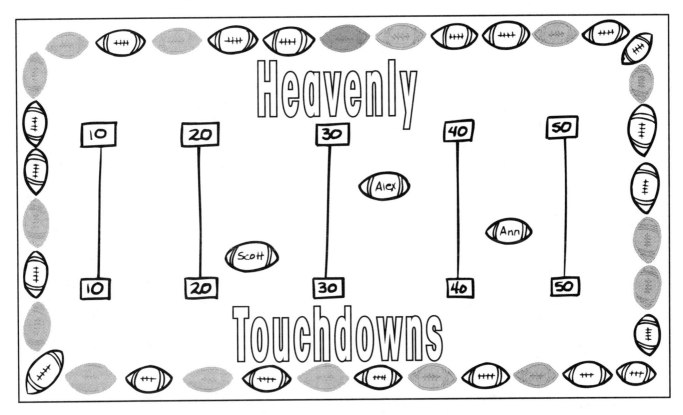

## * Plan

To emphasize the importance of allowing God to lead our lives.

## * Memorize

*Commit to the Lord whatever you do.* Proverbs 16:3

## * Gather

- pattern for footballs and markers from pp. 108-109
- pattern for lettering from p. 110
- pattern for football border from p. 12
- construction paper, white and brown
- felt, green
- yarn, white
- marker, black
- sandpaper

## * Prepare

Duplicate the football pattern on brown paper and the lettering on white paper. Make one football for each child. Duplicate the markers on white paper.

## * Create

1. Attach the green felt to the board for the background. Cut out and attach the football border around the board. Cut out the lettering and post.
2. Divide the board into fifths by vertically attaching white yarn from top to the bottom.

3. Cut out the number markers. Attach the matching numbers sequentially on each end of the white yarn.
4. Cut out a football for each child. Fill in the design on the football and write the child's name on it.
5. Glue a piece of sandpaper to the back of each football. The sandpaper will hold the footballs on the board and allow them to be moveable.
6. Have the children place their footballs on the 10-yardline to begin the game. They may then move their football forward each week for the accomplishment of your choice: Bible verse memorization, attendance or good behavior. Award a small prize to those who reach the 50-yard line.

## * Teach

Say, **When you play a game it is fun to win, isn't it? But if you do not win, does that make the game any less fun to play? God tells us that if we follow Him, we will always be winners in life. That doesn't mean that things in our lives will always happen the way *we* think they should, because we don't know all that God knows. When we follow Him, he will help us to live in the way that He knows is best.**

Suggested Usage: Football season

107

10

20

30

40

50

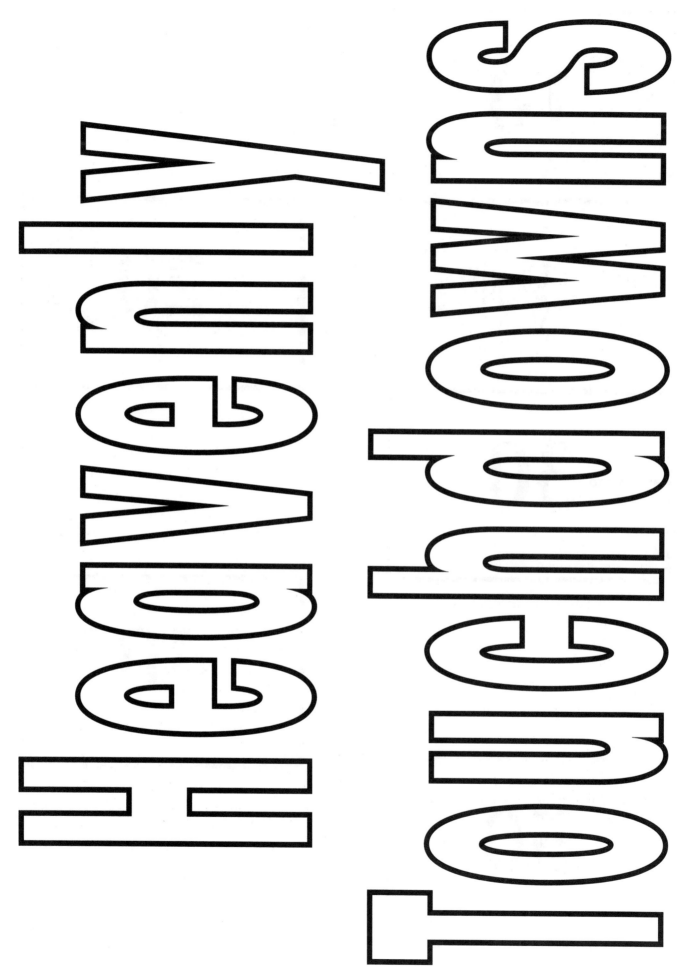

Heavenly

Touchdowns

Jesus Loves The Little Children

Let the little children come to me.
Luke 18:16

* Ages 6-10 *

## * Plan
To recognize that each child is important to Jesus.

## * Memorize
*Let the little children come to me.* Luke 18:16

## * Gather
• patterns for lettering from p. 113-114
• pattern for heart border from p. 13
• pattern for face from p. 112
• construction paper, assorted colors
• poster paper, orange
• black marker
• paper plates
• crayons
• yarn scraps
• glue

## * Prepare
Duplicate the face pattern on a variety of skin tone-colored paper, one for each child, and the lettering on various colors of paper.

## * Create
1. Cover the bulletin board with orange background paper. Cut out the lettering and attach it to the board. Write the memory verse on the bottom of board with black marker.
2. Cut and accordion fold strips of different colors of construction paper according to the instant border directions on page 10. Trace the heart border pattern and cut out the border. Staple the border around the edges of the board.
3. Give each student a face pattern, a paper plate, yarn and construction paper scraps. Have the students cut out and color the face pattern and fold it in half along the dashed lines.
4. Inside the face, have the children write a few sentences about themselves—preferences, hobbies or family member names.
5. Have the students glue the bottom half of the face to the center of the plate, then decorate the plates with yarn scraps to make hair.
6. Attach the faces to the bulletin board.

## * Teach
Say, **Did you know that Jesus especially loves children? He knows everything about you, even the number of hairs on your heads!** (Matt. 10:30) Allow the children to try counting the hairs on their heads. **Do we even know the exact number of hairs on our heads? No! That's why we should turn to Jesus with our problems—He knows more about us than we even know about ourselves.**

Suggested Usage: General

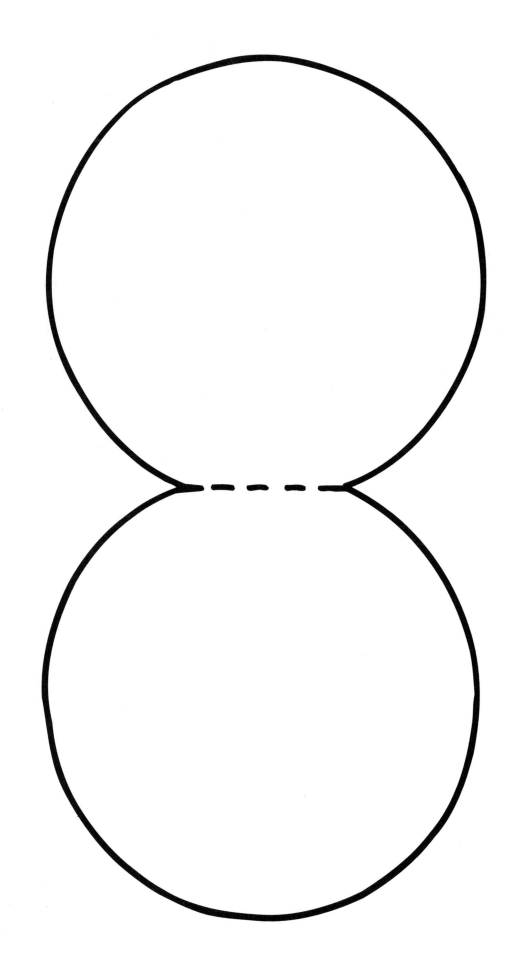

# The Little Children

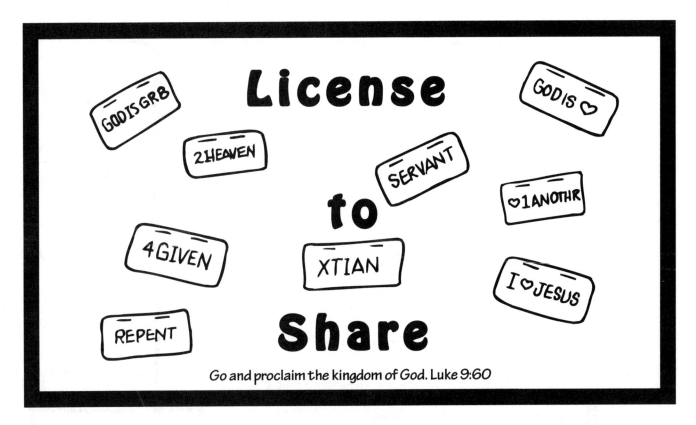

**Ages 6-10**

**✳ Plan**

To emphasize the call to share the Good News.

**✳ Memorize**

*Go and proclaim the kingdom of God.* Luke 9:60

**✳ Gather**

• pattern for license plate from p. 116
• pattern for lettering from p. 117
• paper, white
• construction paper, black
• poster paper, yellow
• crayons
• safety scissors

**✳ Prepare**

Duplicate the license plate on white paper and the lettering on black construction paper. For the border, cut several 1" wide strips of black construction paper.

**✳ Create**

1. Cover the bulletin board with yellow background paper. Cut out the lettering and attach it.
2. For the border, staple the 1" strips along the board's edges, about 1" from all edges.

3. Discuss with the class the concept of "vanity" plates—license plates that use abbreviated spelling and numbers to make a statement. Ask the students to share any they have seen. Then distribute the duplicated license plates and have the class use crayons and scissors to design, cut out and color a license plate that proclaims their love for God. See the examples above for ideas.
4. Attach the license plates on the bulletin board. (Optional idea: use the colors of your state's license plate for the board's colors!)

**✳ Teach**

After you remove the bulletin board, cover the license plates with clear, self-stick plastic and allow the students to take them home. Say, **Ask your parents if you may hang your license plate in your family's car or tape it to your bike.**

Suggested Usage: General

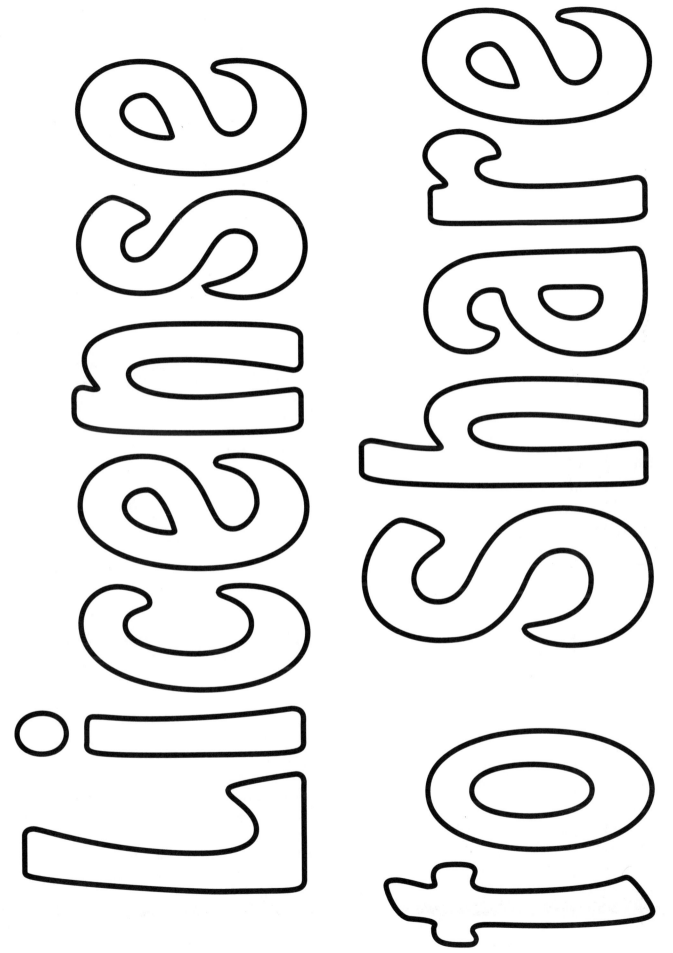

License to share

## ✷ Plan

To reinforce that we grow through following God.

## ✷ Memorize

*I can do everything through him who gives me strength.* Philippians 4:13

## ✷ Gather

- pattern for arrows from p. 119
- pattern for lettering from p. 120
- pattern for V-shaped border from p. 11
- construction paper, various colors
- poster paper, yellow
- felt, red or orange
- marker, black
- crayons
- aluminum foil
- sandpaper
- glue

## ✷ Prepare

Duplicate one arrow for each child on various colors of paper, and the lettering on red paper.

## ✷ Create

1. Attach the yellow paper to the bulletin board. Cut out and post the lettering.
2. Cut and fold strips of brown paper according to the instant border directions on page 10. Trace the border onto the folded paper and cut out. Staple the border around the board's edges.
3. Cut a large circle from felt for a target. Draw four circles on the felt using black marker. Attach the target to the center of the board.
4. Cut out the arrows. Write each child's name on one.
5. Distribute small pieces of foil for the class to glue to the tips of their arrows. Show how to glue a piece of sandpaper to the back of each arrow.
6. Cut out five squares and write the numbers 10, 20, 30, 40 and 50 on them. Attach to the circles as shown.
7. Have the children place their arrows on the outside ring. Each week they say the memory verse they may move their arrow to the next ring.

## ✷ Teach

Say, **If you were using a real dart board you would need to be strong to throw the arrows. God says that He will make us strong, not just in our bodies but also in our Christian life.** To further illustrate the lesson, cut a circle out of the center of a cardboard box. Have the students take turns tossing bean bags in the box. Say, **See how well you can throw the bean bags through the hole? When you were younger you would not have been able to do that! God is helping you to grow and learn so that you can live for Him.**

Suggested Usage: General

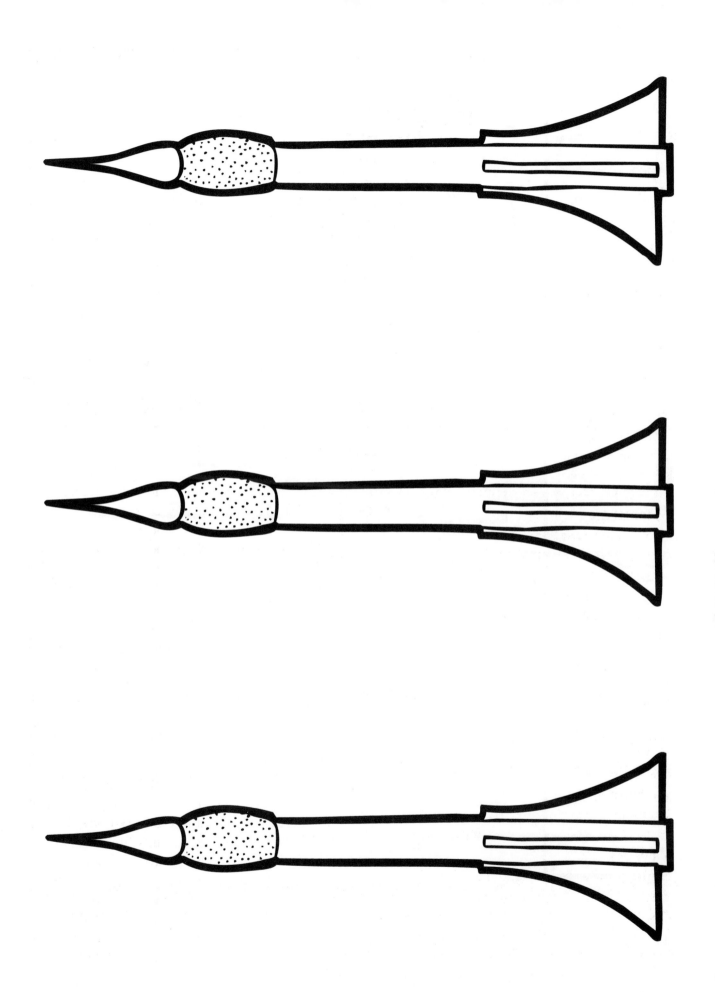

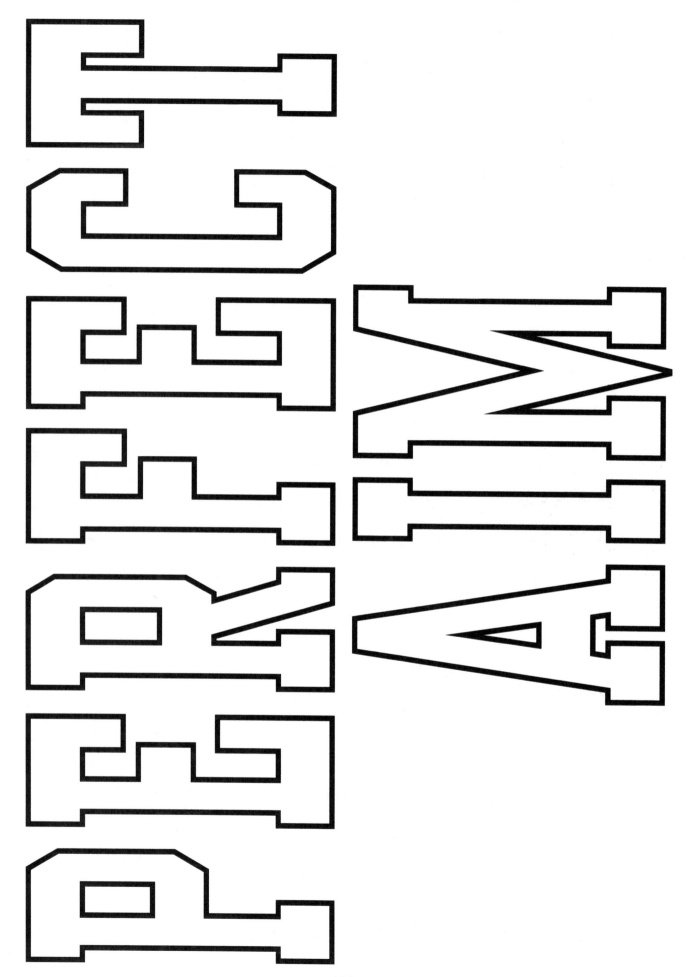

120

# Squirrels and Acorns

For God so loved the world that he gave his one and only Son, that whoever believes in him shall not perish but have eternal life. John 3:16

✳ **Ages 6-10** ✳

### ✳ Plan
To understand the biblical base for salvation.

### ✳ Memorize
*For God so loved the world that he gave his one and only Son, that whoever believes in him shall not perish but have eternal life.* John 3:16

### ✳ Gather
• pattern for lettering from p. 124
• pattern for acorn border from p. 11
• patterns for squirrel and nut from pp. 122-123
• construction paper, black and shades of brown
• poster paper, orange or yellow
• marker, black
• clear, self-stick plastic
• push pin
• plastic sandwich bag
• Velcro
• nuts

### ✳ Prepare
Duplicate the lettering on black paper. Duplicate six squirrels on dark brown paper and six nuts on light brown paper.

### ✳ Create
1. Cover the bulletin board with orange or yellow paper. Cut out the lettering and attach it to the board. Use a black marker to write the memory verse at the bottom of the board.

2. Cut and fold strips of brown paper according to the instant border directions on page 10. Trace the acorn border onto the folded paper and cut out. Post the border around the board's edges.

3. Cut out the squirrels. Write one of the questions from p. 122 on each one. Cover the squirrels with self-stick plastic and attach them to the board.

4. Cut out the acorns. On each one, write a Bible verse answer from p. 122. On the backs write the number of the question that goes with the verse. Cover the acorns with self-stick plastic and store them in a plastic sandwich bag attached with a push pin to the board.

5. Place a piece of Velcro on the squirrels' paws and the corresponding pieces on the acorns.

6. Challenge the students to answer the questions by finding the correct acorn and attaching it to the squirrels' paws. The students may check their answers by looking at the backs of the acorns.

### ✳ Teach
Ask the questions on the squirrels and allow the students to answer, then read the acorns and have them tell which acorns fit with which squirrels. Split the class into pairs and have them memorize the Bible verse. After each pair correctly repeats the verse to you, give them a handful of nuts to eat.

Suggested Usage: General

121

# Questions and Answers for Squirrels and Acorns

**1.** What is sin?

**2.** Who sins?

**3.** Who saves me from sin?

**4.** How do I become a Christian?

**5.** Why do I need to become a Christian?

**6.** How can I be sure I am Christian?

## Answers

1. All wrong doing is sin. 1 John 5:17

2. All have sinned and fall short of the glory of God. Romans 3:23

3. Look, the Lamb of God [Jesus], who takes away the sin of the world! John 1:29

4. For God so loved the world that he gave his one and only Son, that whoever believes in him shall not perish but have eternal life. John 3:16

5. If we claim to be without sin, we deceive ourselves and the truth is not in us. 1 John 1:8

6. Whoever believes in the Son has eternal life. John 3:36

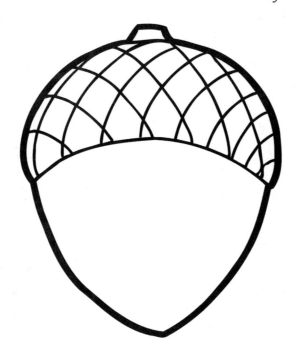

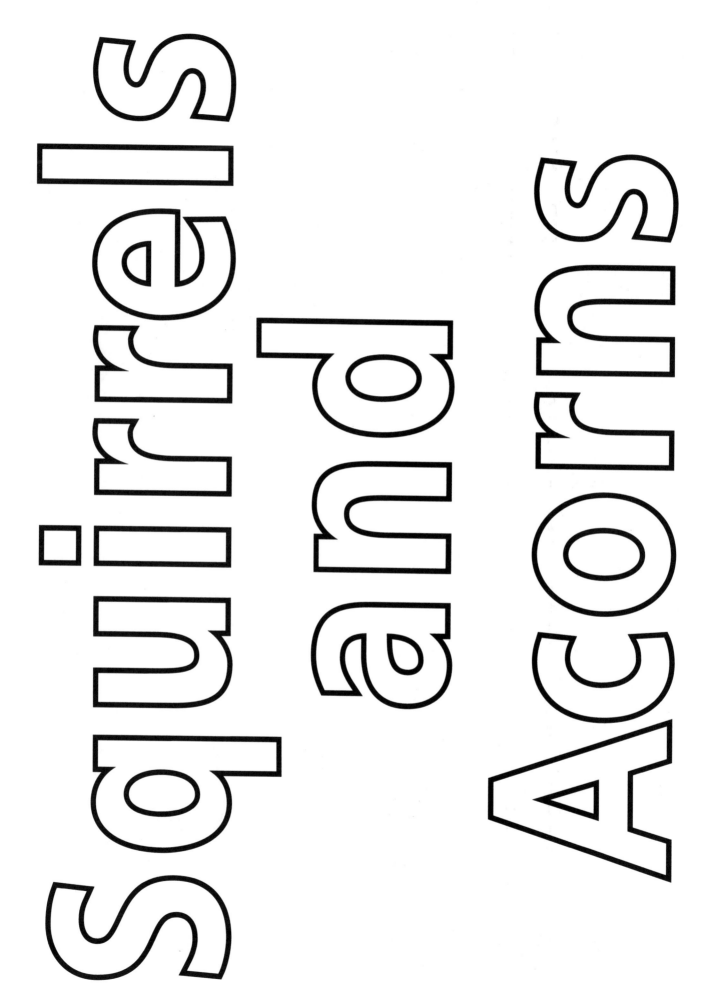

squirrels and
Acorns

The righteous are as bold as a lion. Proverbs 28:1

## ✴ Ages 6-10 ✴

### ✴ Plan
To recognize Bible characters as worthy of admiration.

### ✴ Memorize
*The righteous are as bold as a lion.* Proverbs 28:1

### ✴ Gather
• pattern for lettering from p. 127
• pattern for stamp from p. 126
• pattern for stamp edge border from p. 13
• construction paper, black and white
• poster paper, red
• marker, black
• crayons

### ✴ Prepare
Duplicate the lettering on black construction paper and one large stamp per student on white paper.

### ✴ Create
1. Cover the bulletin board with red background paper. Cut out the lettering and attach it to the board in the top center. Use a black marker to write the memory verse at the bottom of the board.
2. Cut and fold strips of white construction paper according to the instant border directions on page 10. Trace the stamp edge border pattern and cut out the border. Staple the border around the edges of the bulletin board.
3. Discuss with the students the tradition of using important people on commemorative stamps. (Bring in some samples if possible.) Ask the students to select a person from the Bible they admire the most—someone they think belongs on a stamp.
4. Have the children cut out the stamps and use crayons to design and color a stamp for their chosen Bible character.
5. Attach the completed stamps to the board.

### ✴ Teach
Have the students share the stamps with the class and explain why they selected the people on their stamps. Or, have each student name the person on his or her stamp and allow the other students to call out information on that person. For example, if someone says "Noah," the class may say, "Built an ark" or "Was obedient to God."

Suggested Usage: General